FIGURATIVE COLLECTION 2020
Volume I

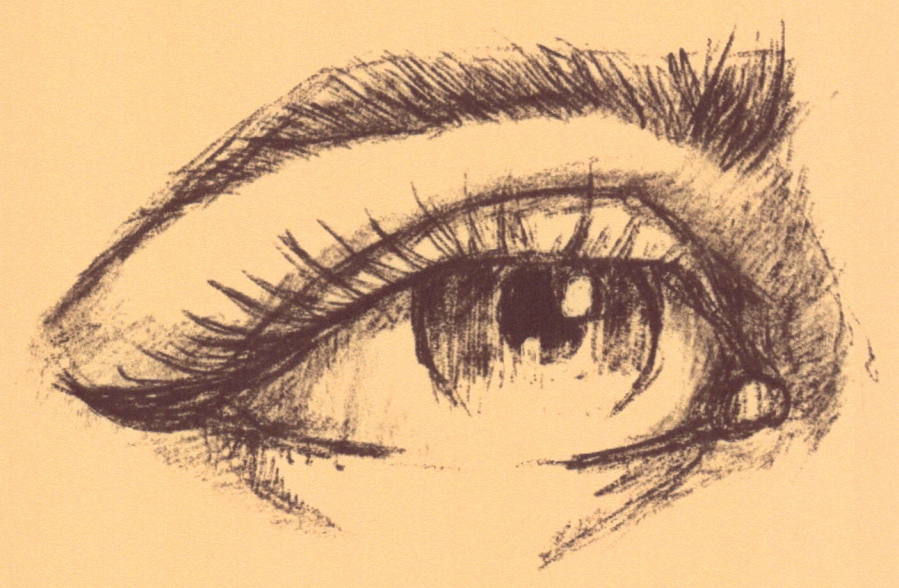

BHARADWAJ BALRAJ

Dedicated to my mom and my wife for their relentless support
Also to my little sister and brother for nudging me whenever I fall out of balance

Also to my unborn child playing in momma's belly

Welcome Note

Dear Reader,

    I want to thank you from the bottom of my heart for purchasing my figurative collection 2020, Volume I book. You are now in possession of something very close to my heart that I created with a lot of passion.

    What makes this book special is that I restarted my drawing after a 4 year gap. After 100 continuous days of drawing, amidst COVID-19 struggles, I was able to buck up my confidence in figure drawing. This book contains handpicked high resolution collection from my everyday sketches and a peek into my drawing process.

    I sincerely hope that each page of this book provides you the same excitement with which I created them.

Thanks,
Bharad.

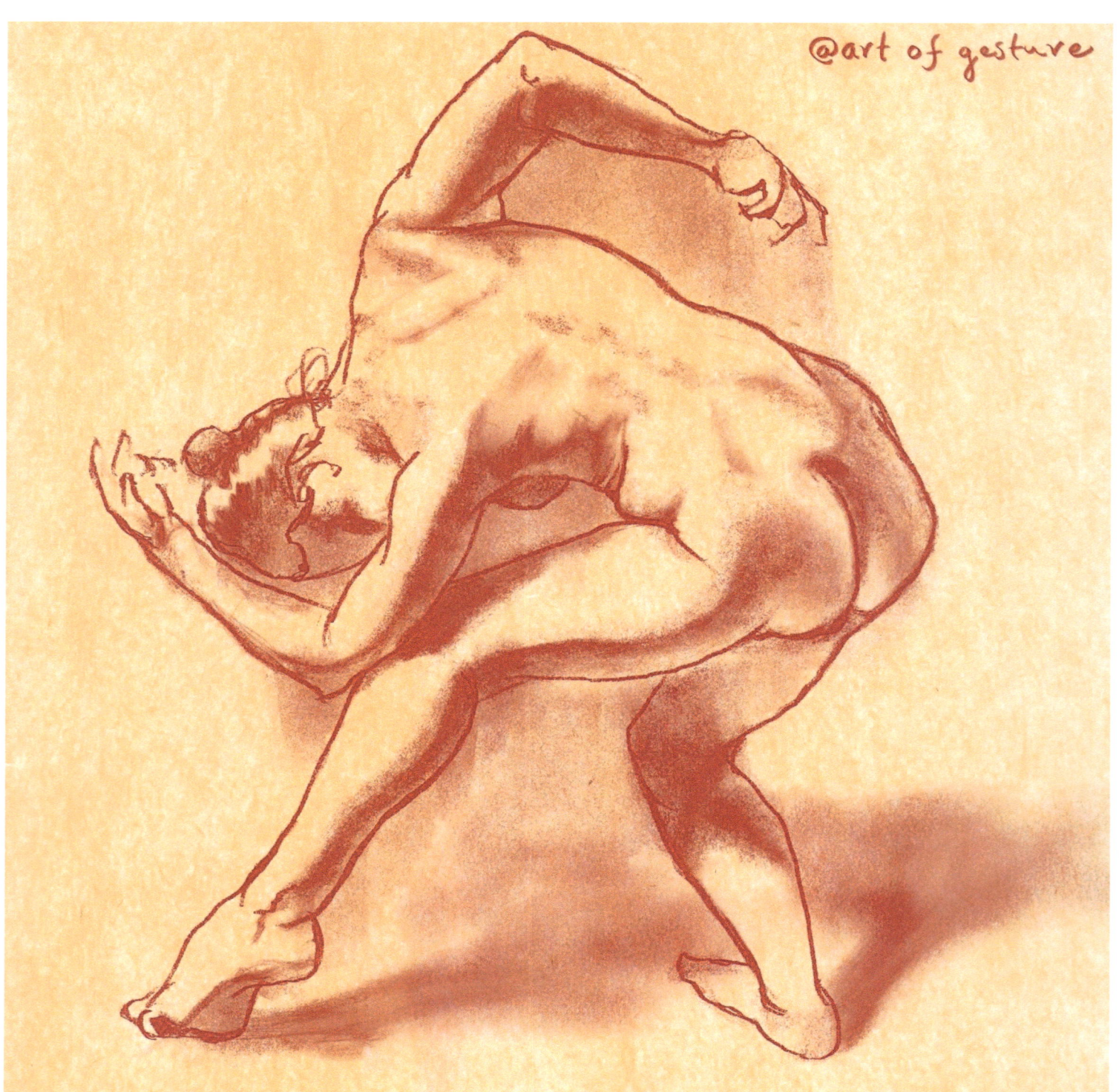

@art of gesture

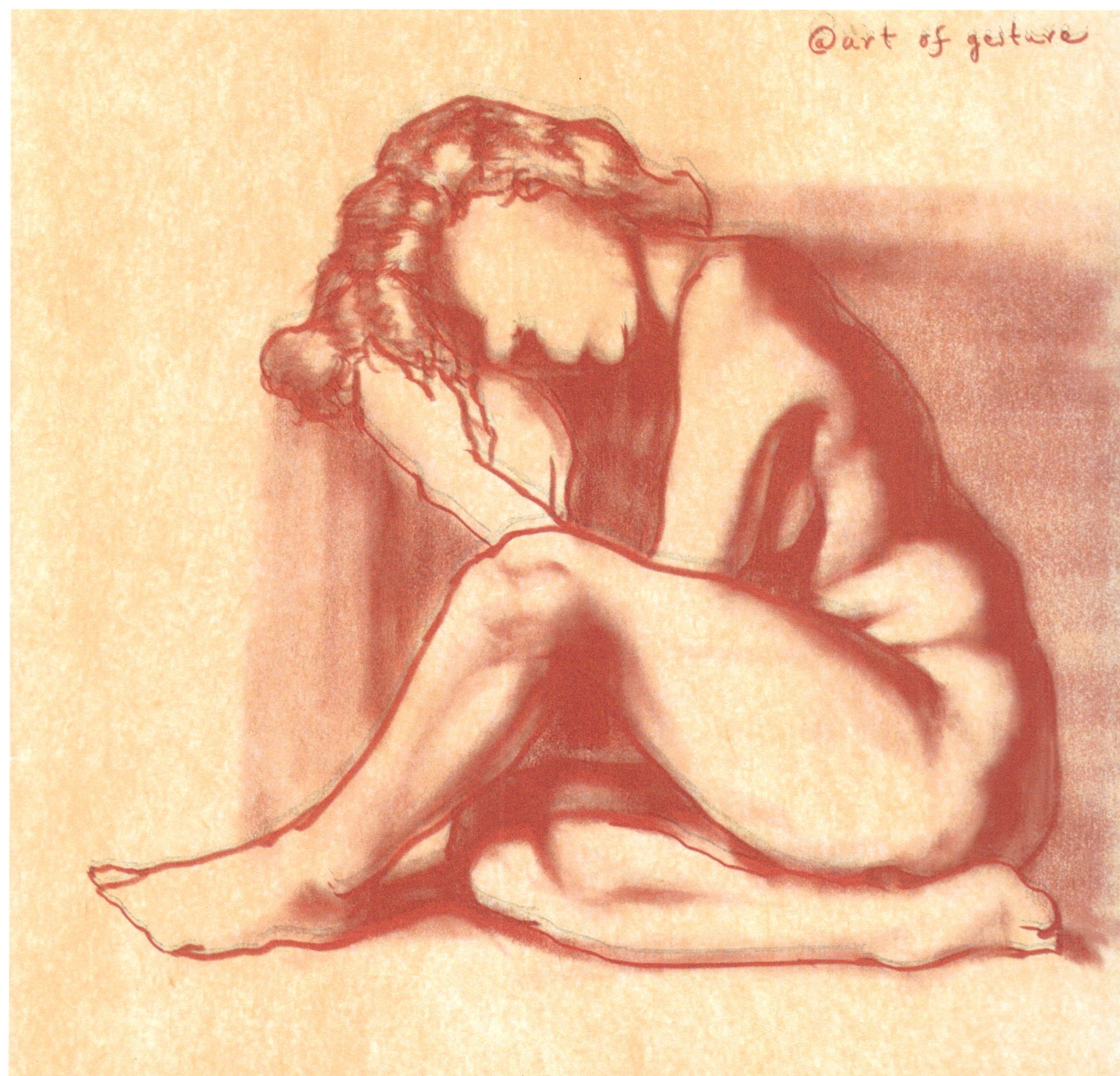

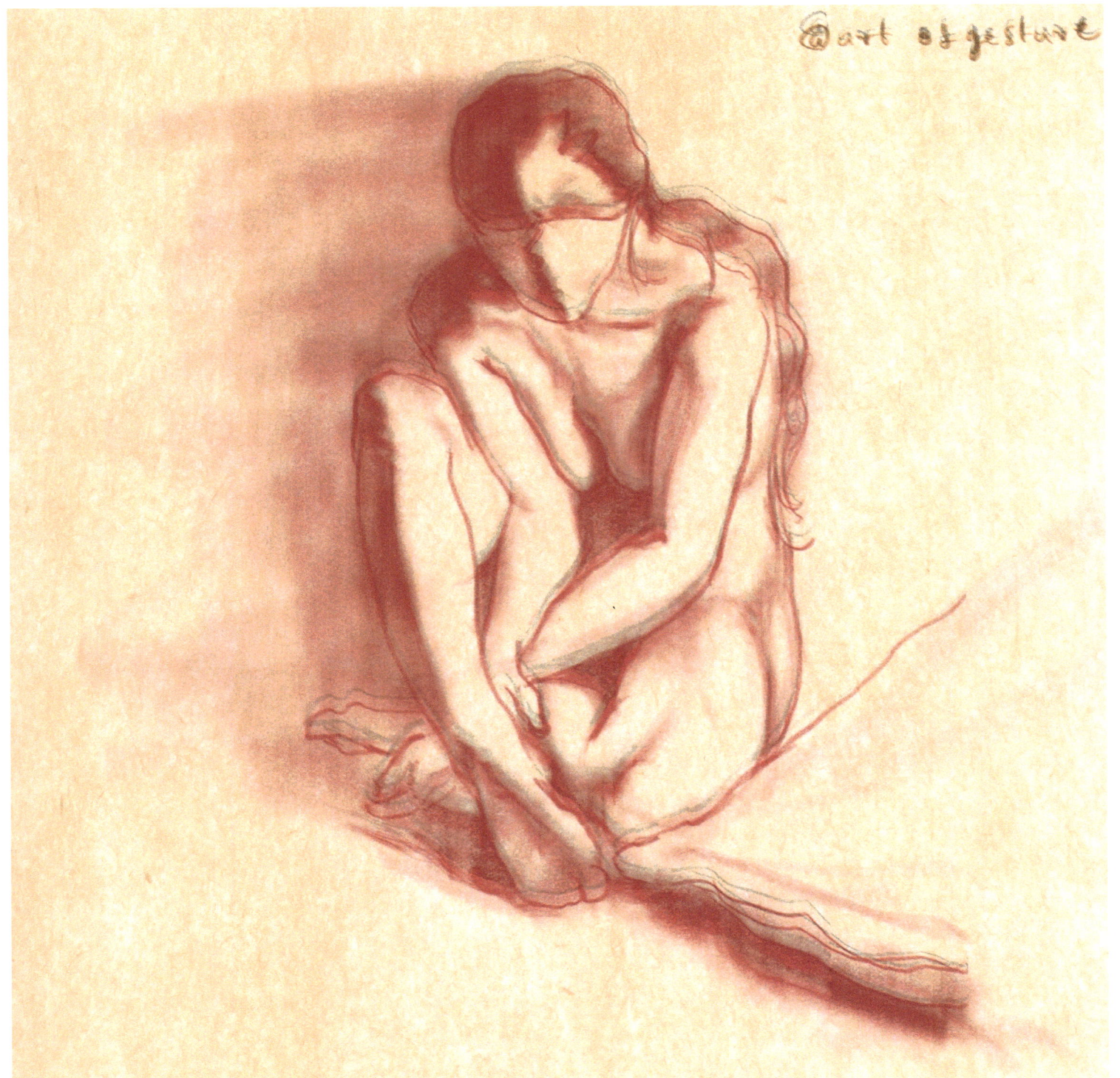

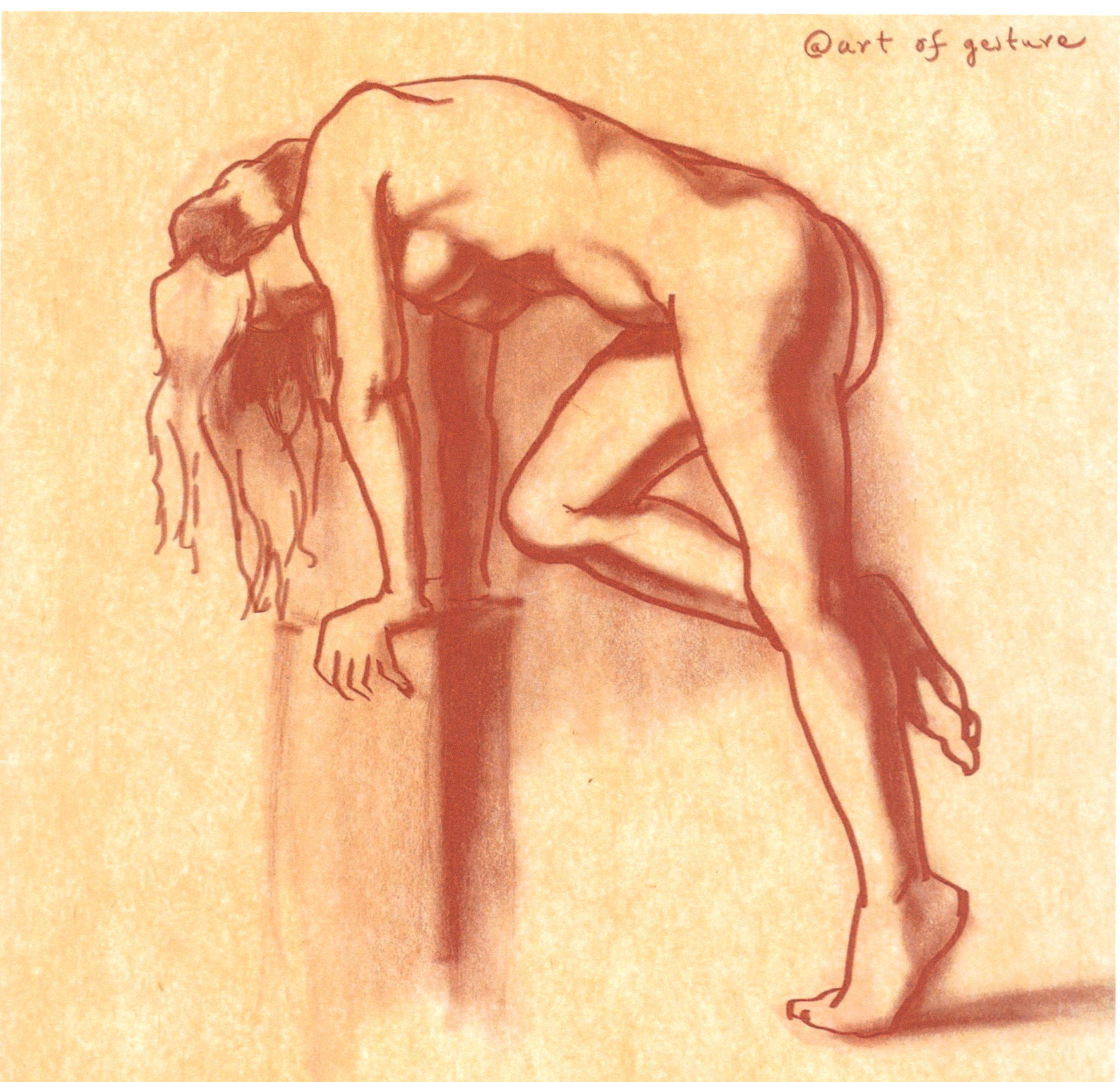

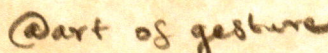
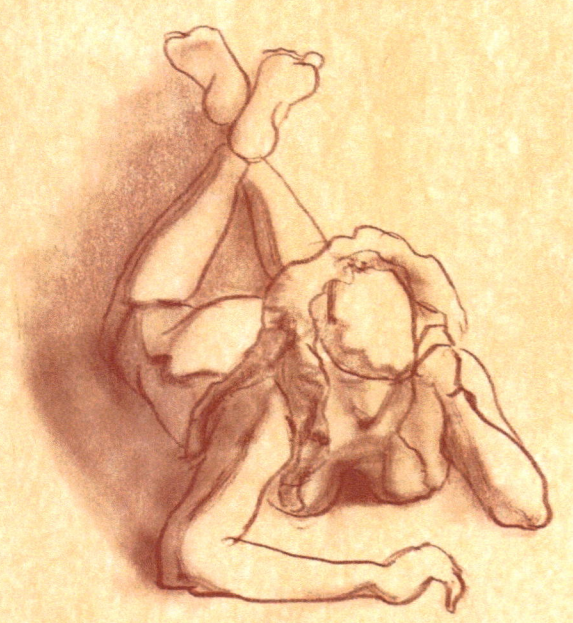
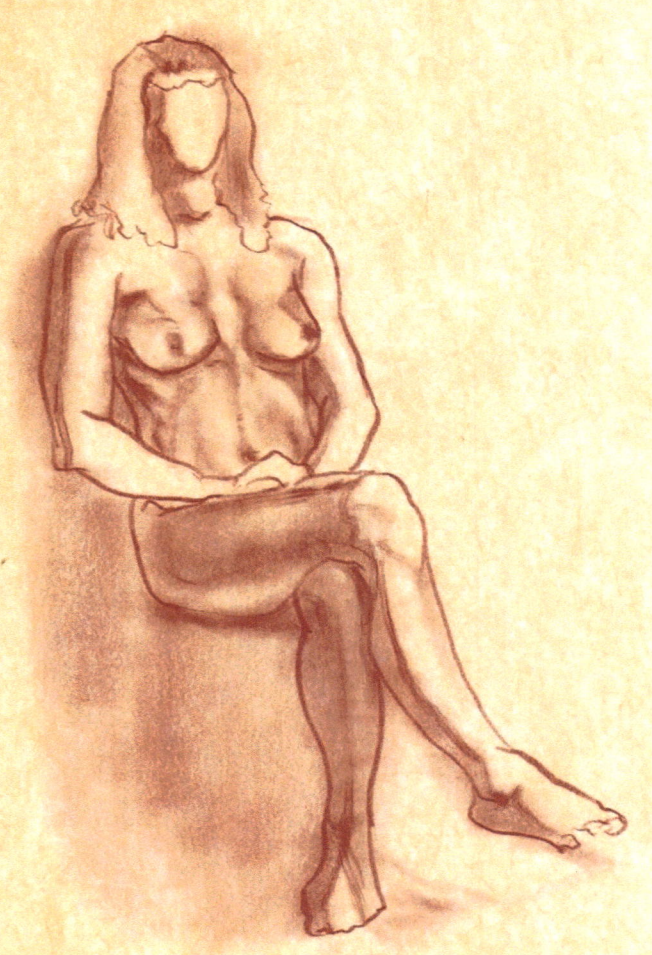

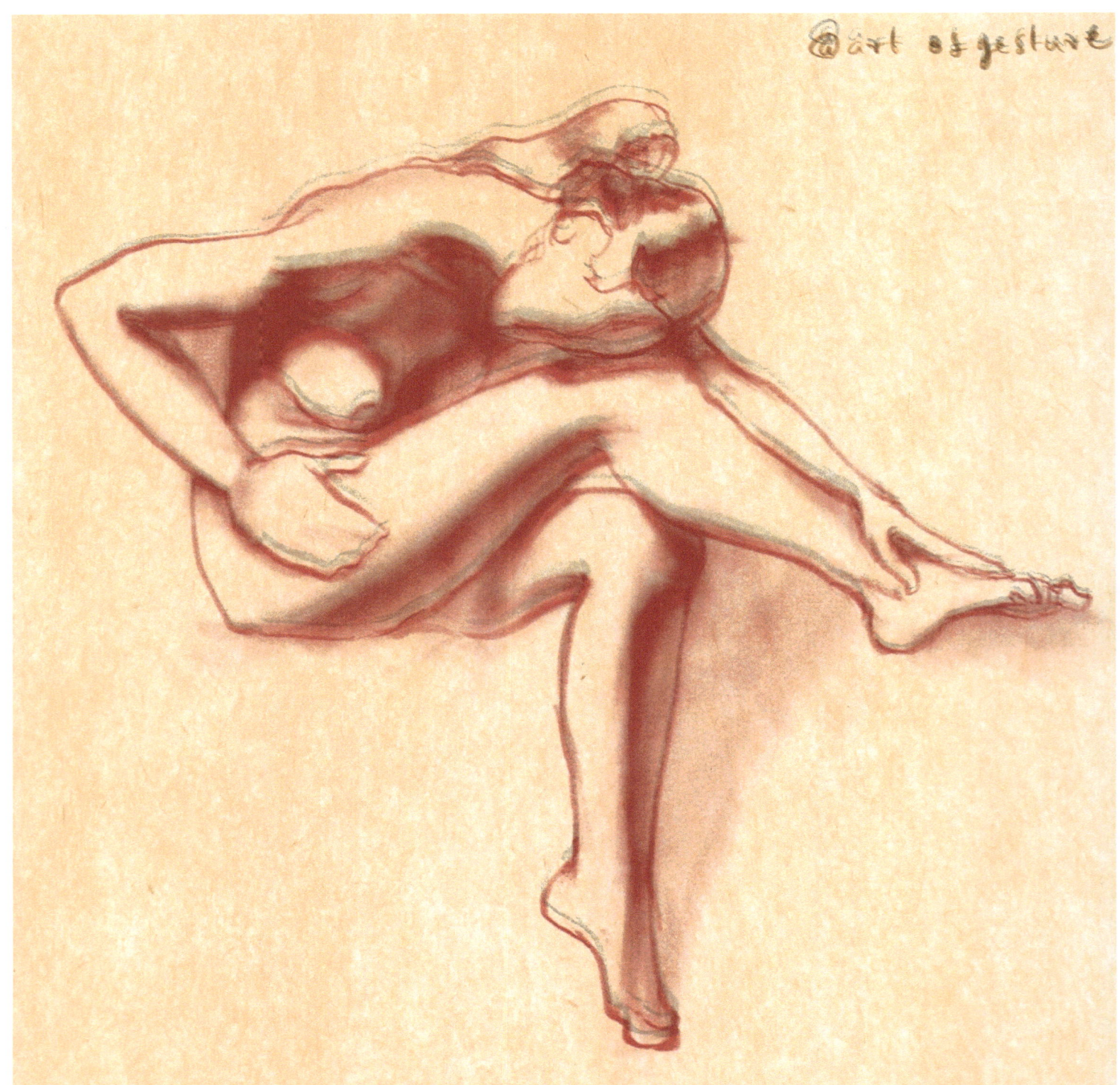

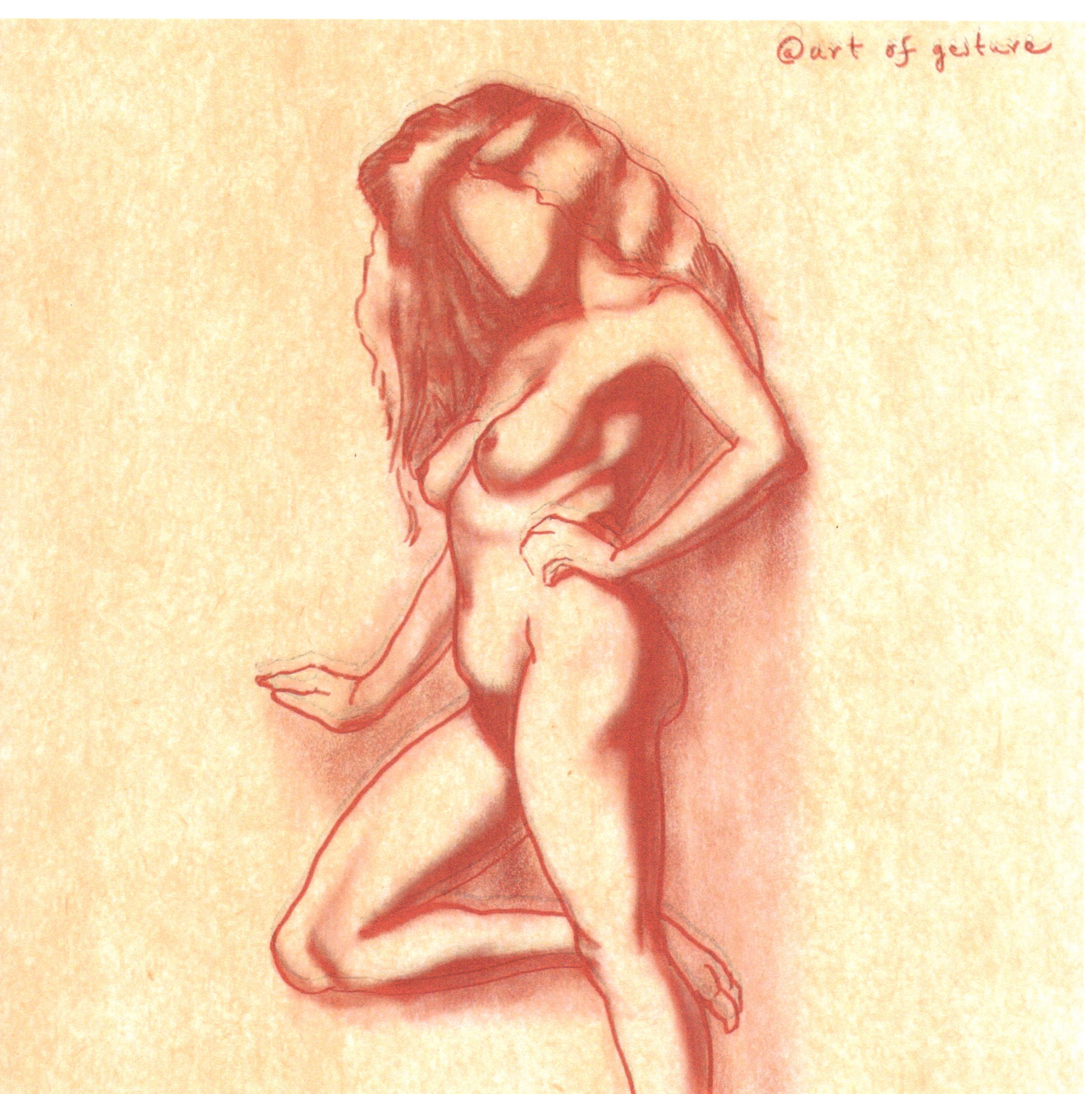

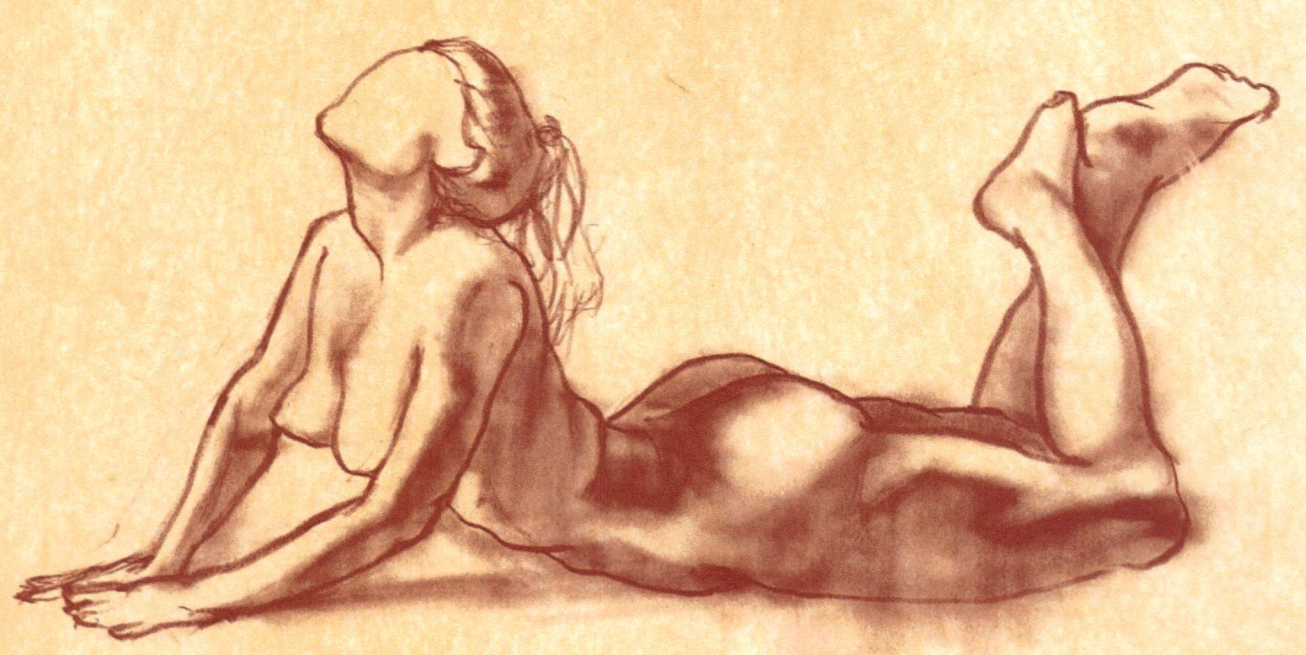

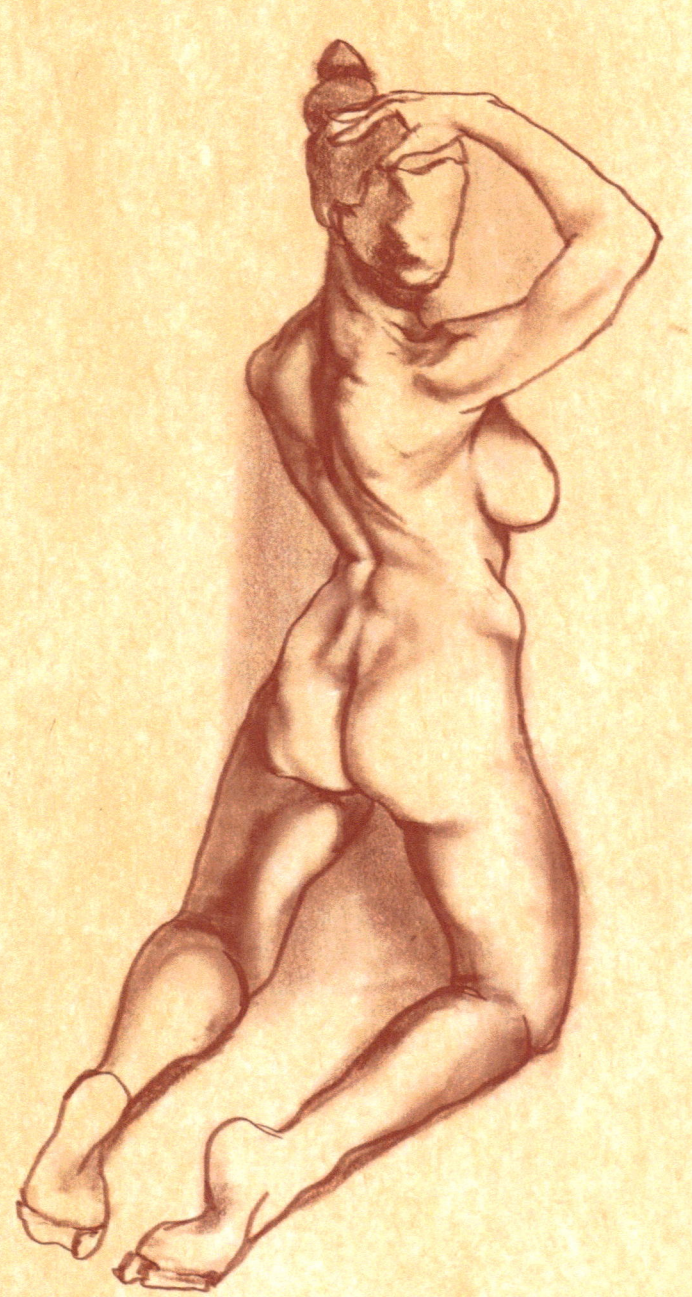

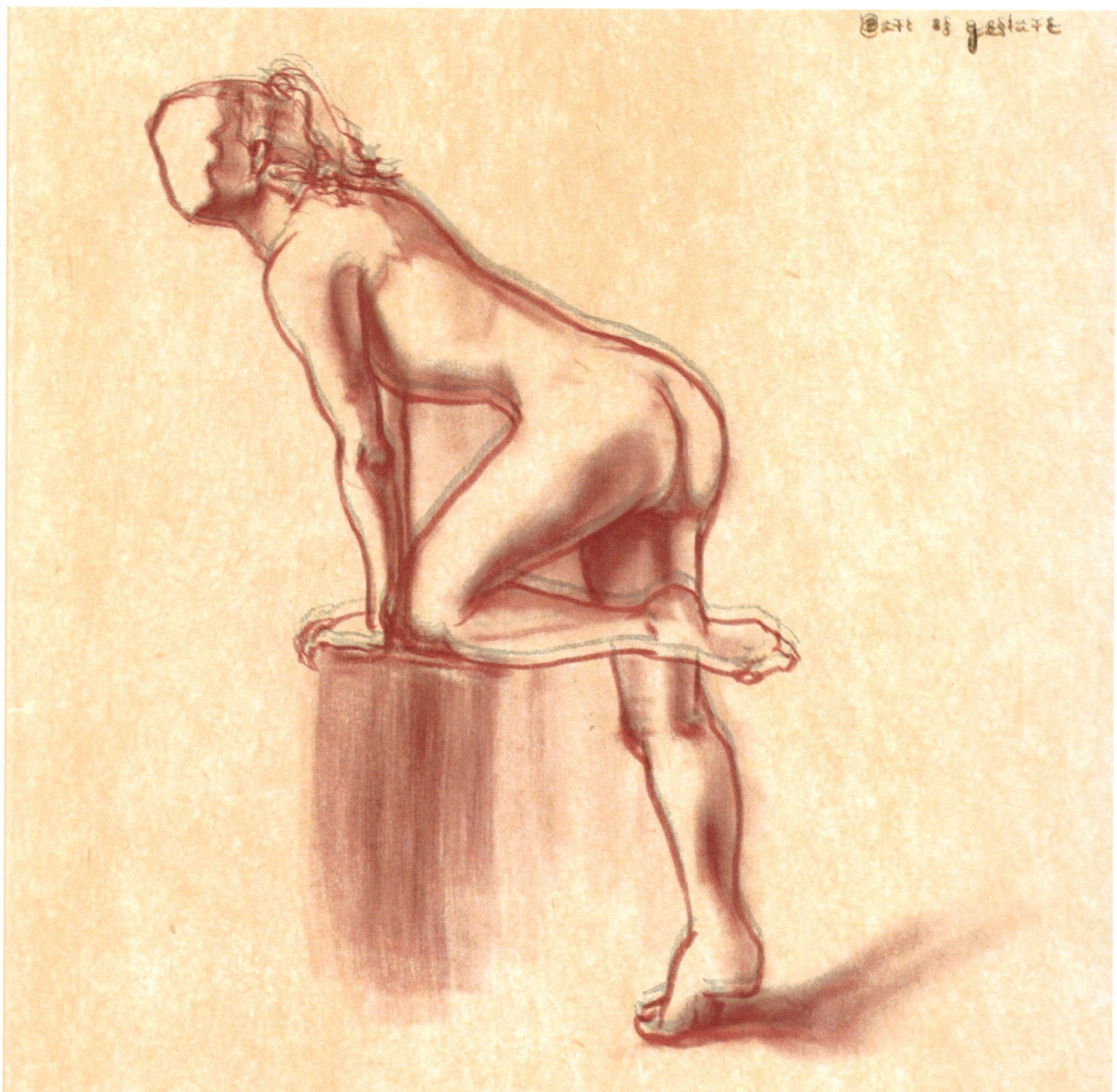

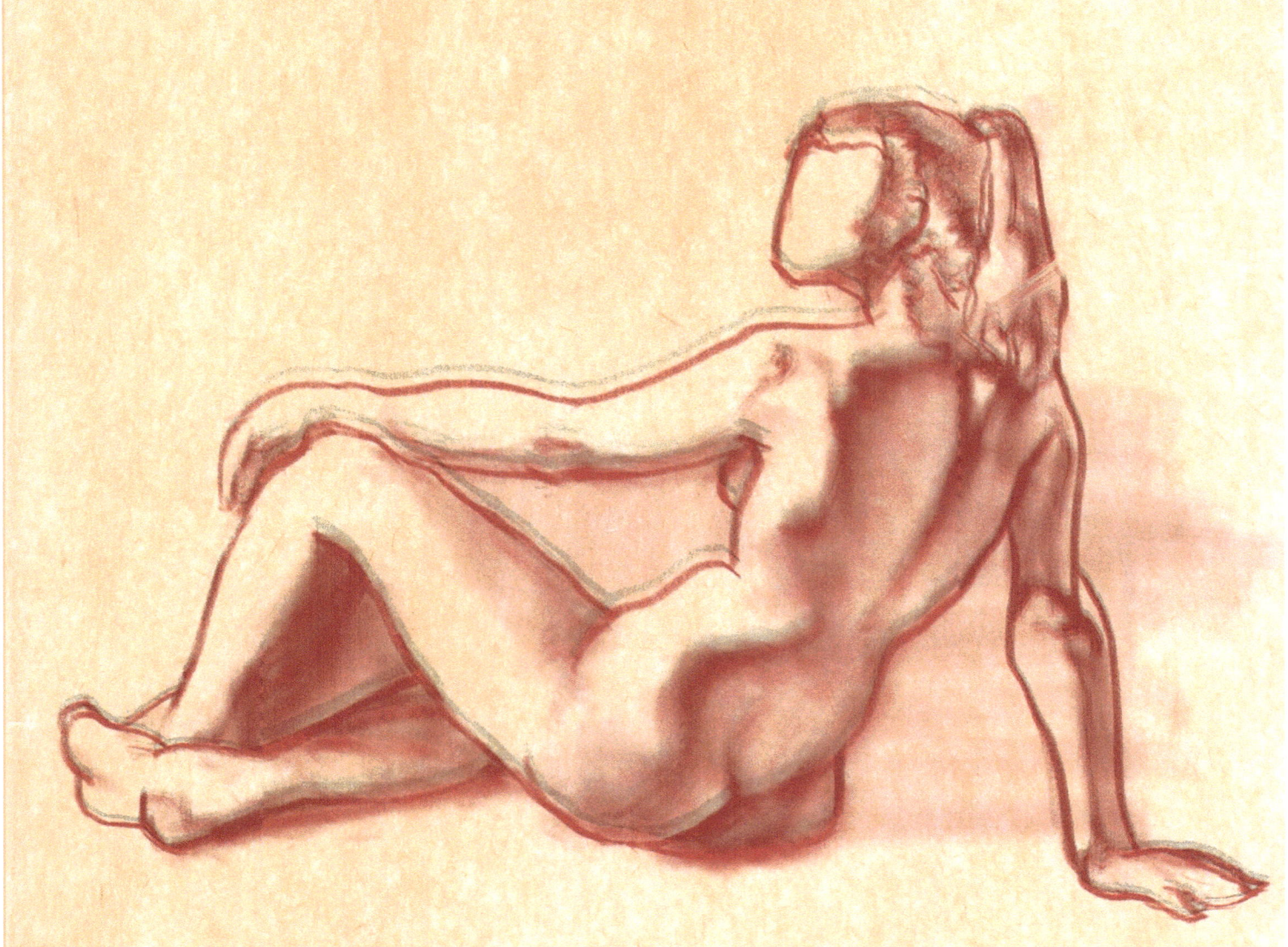

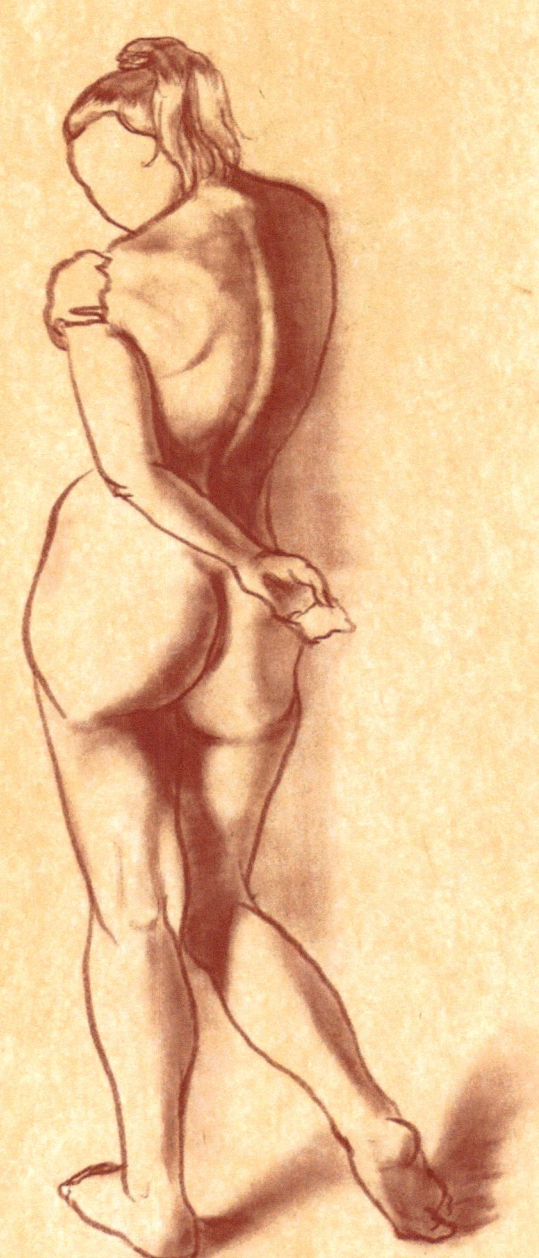

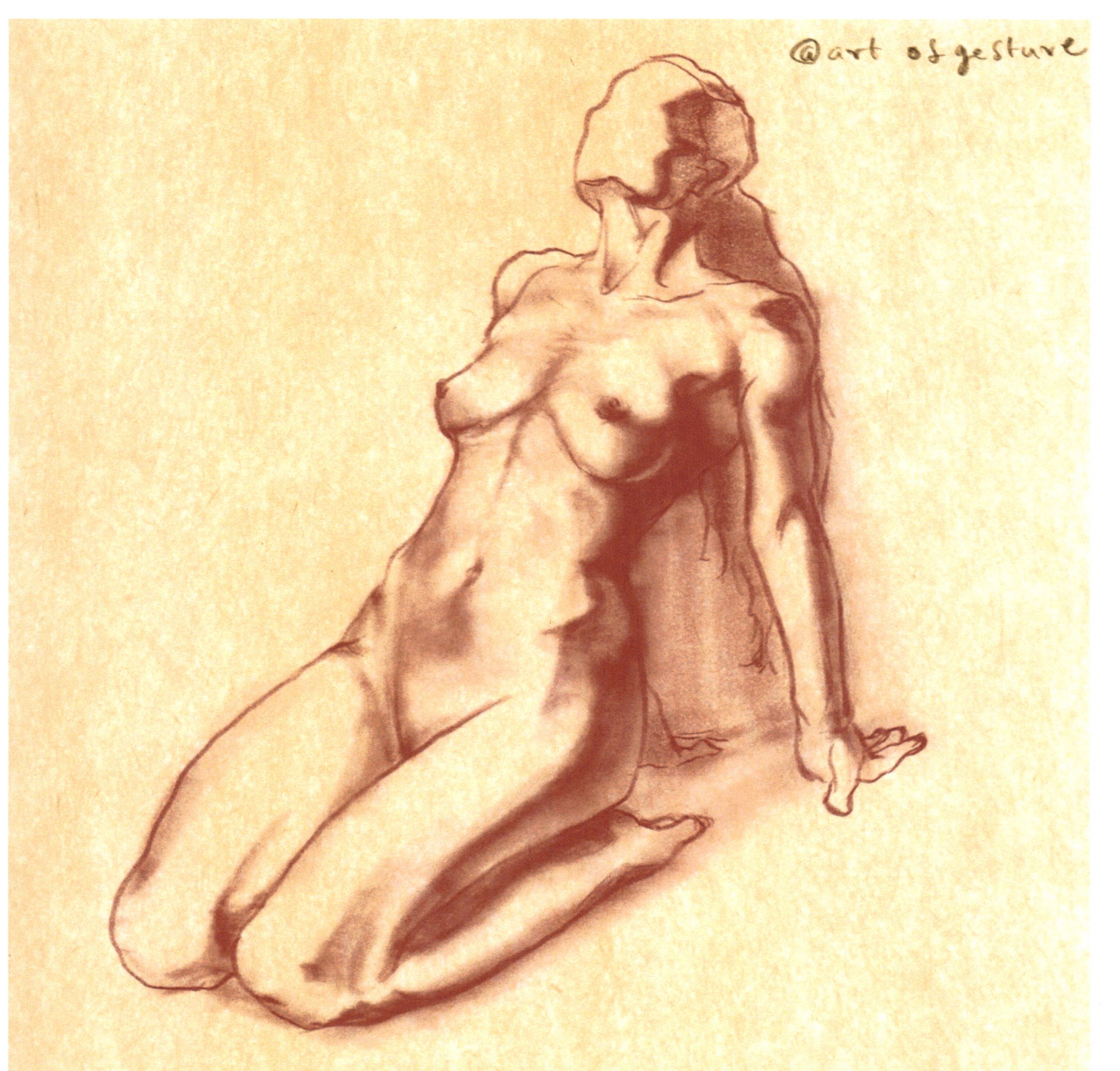

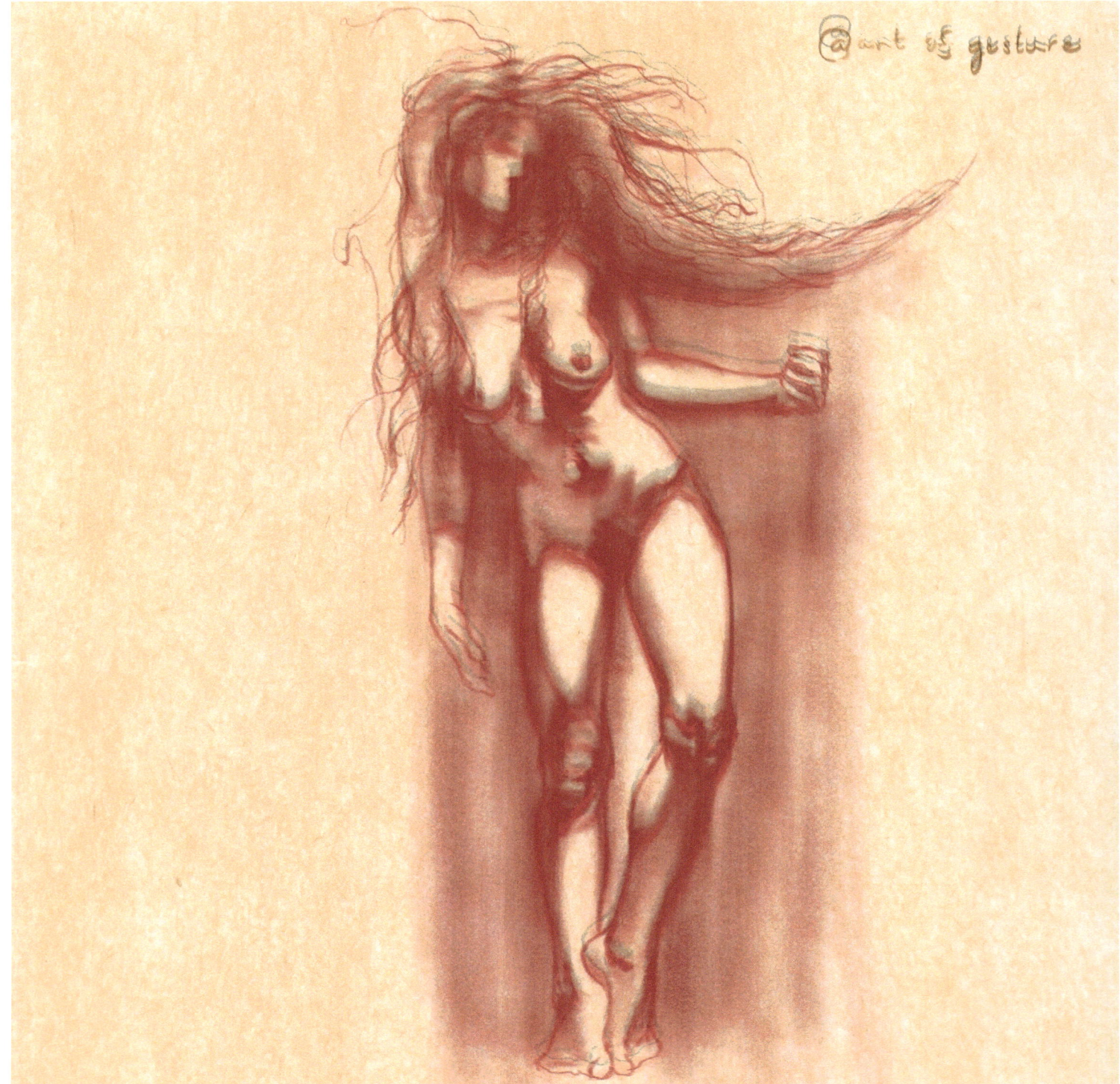

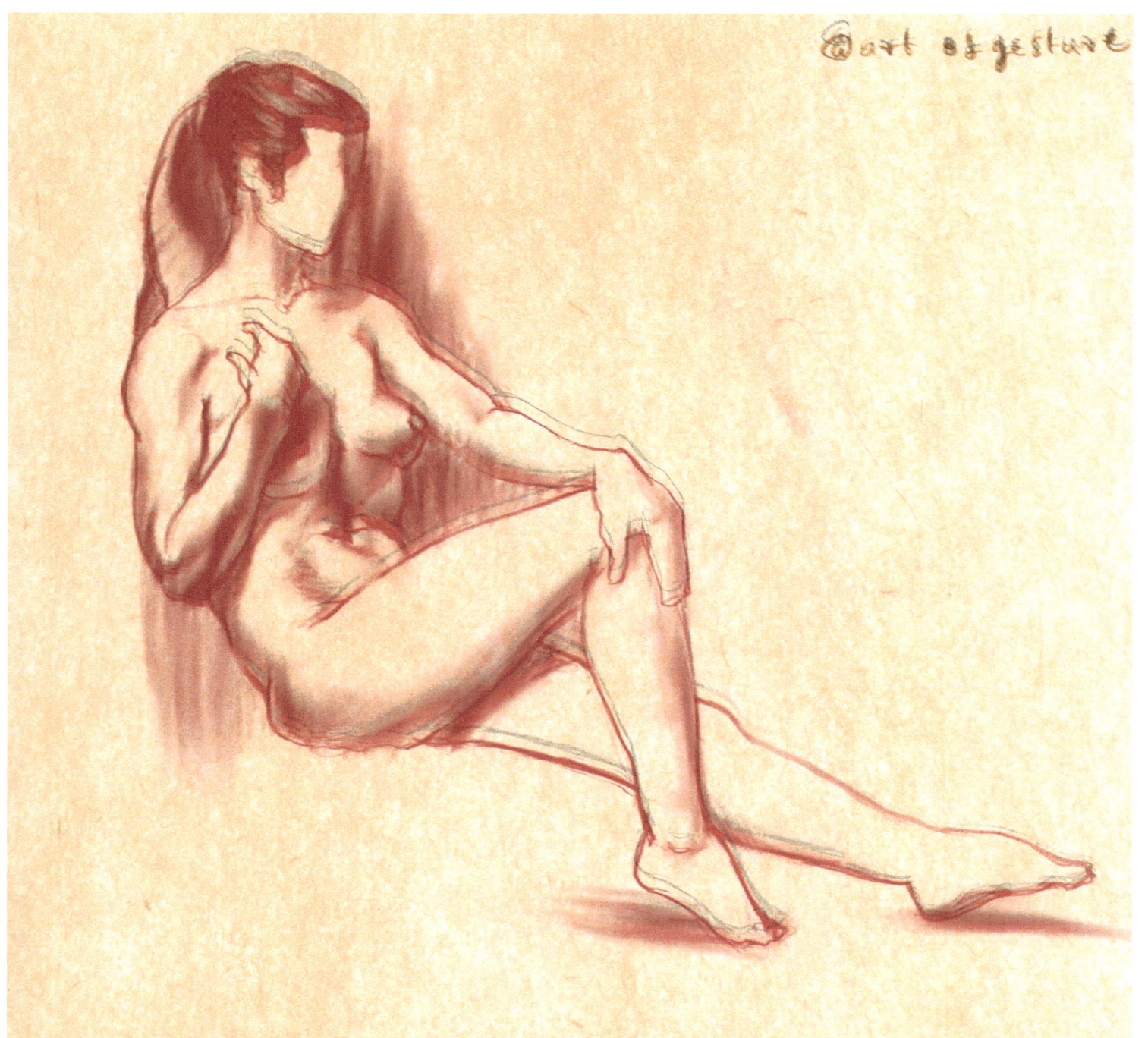

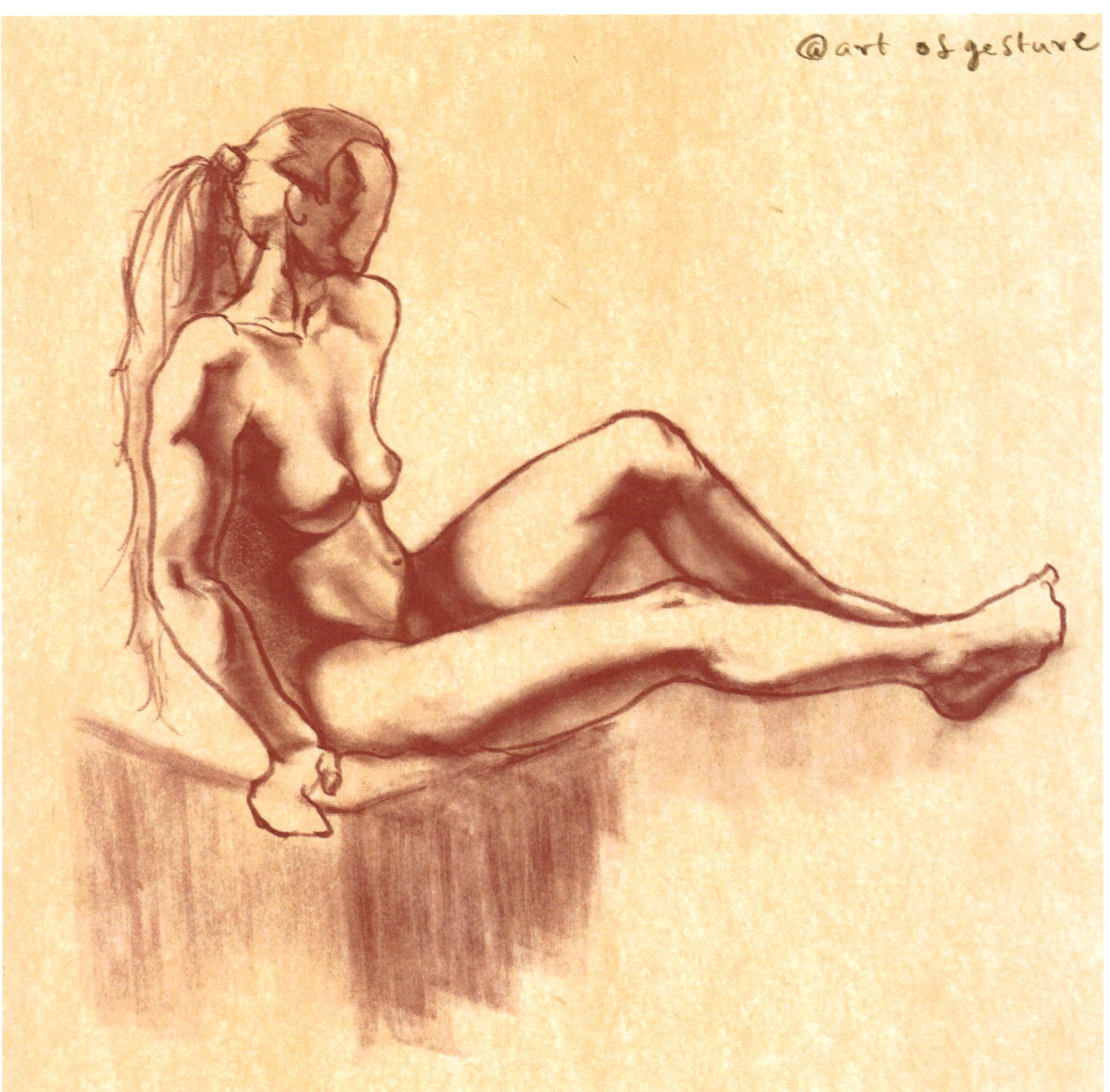

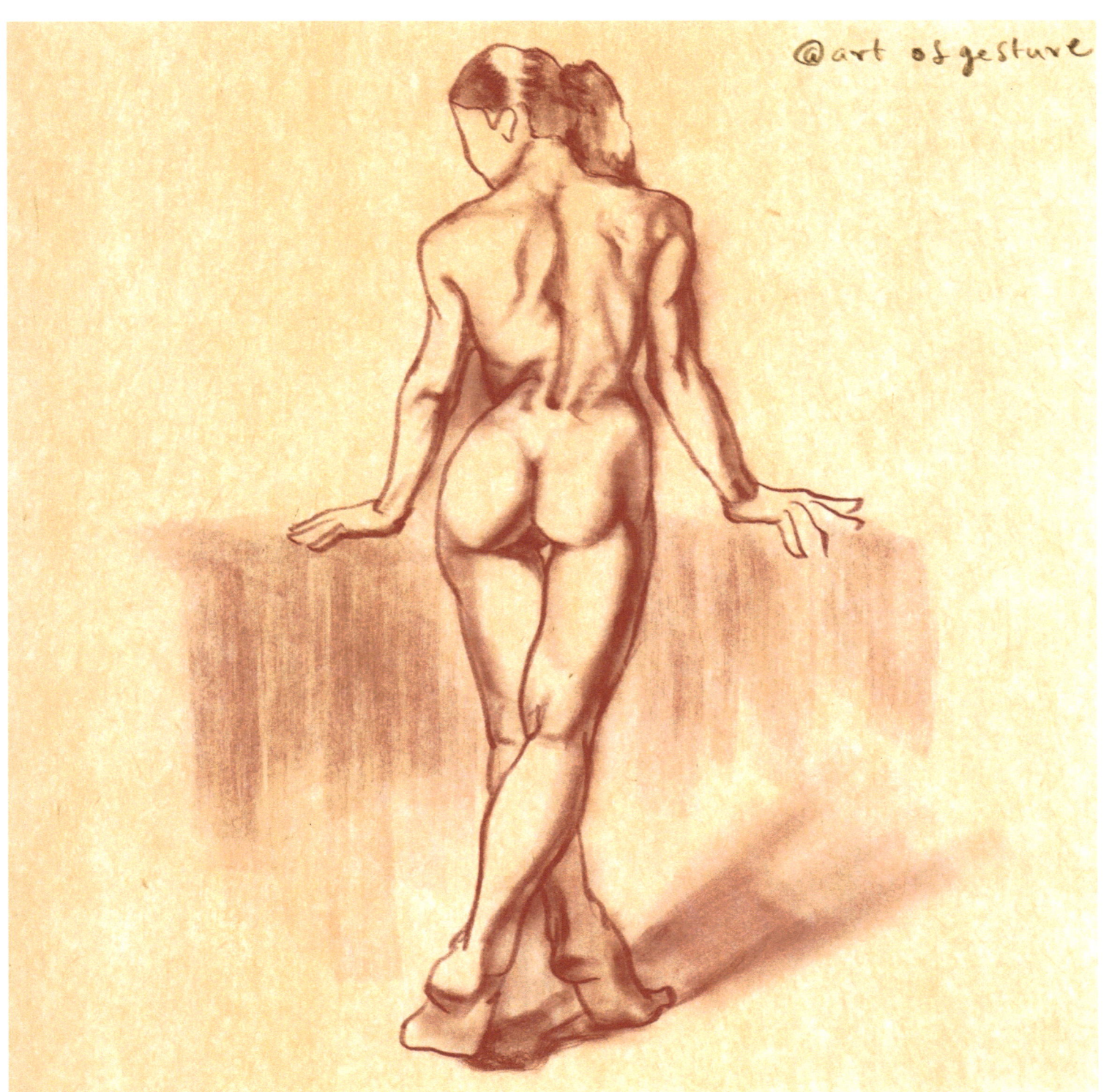

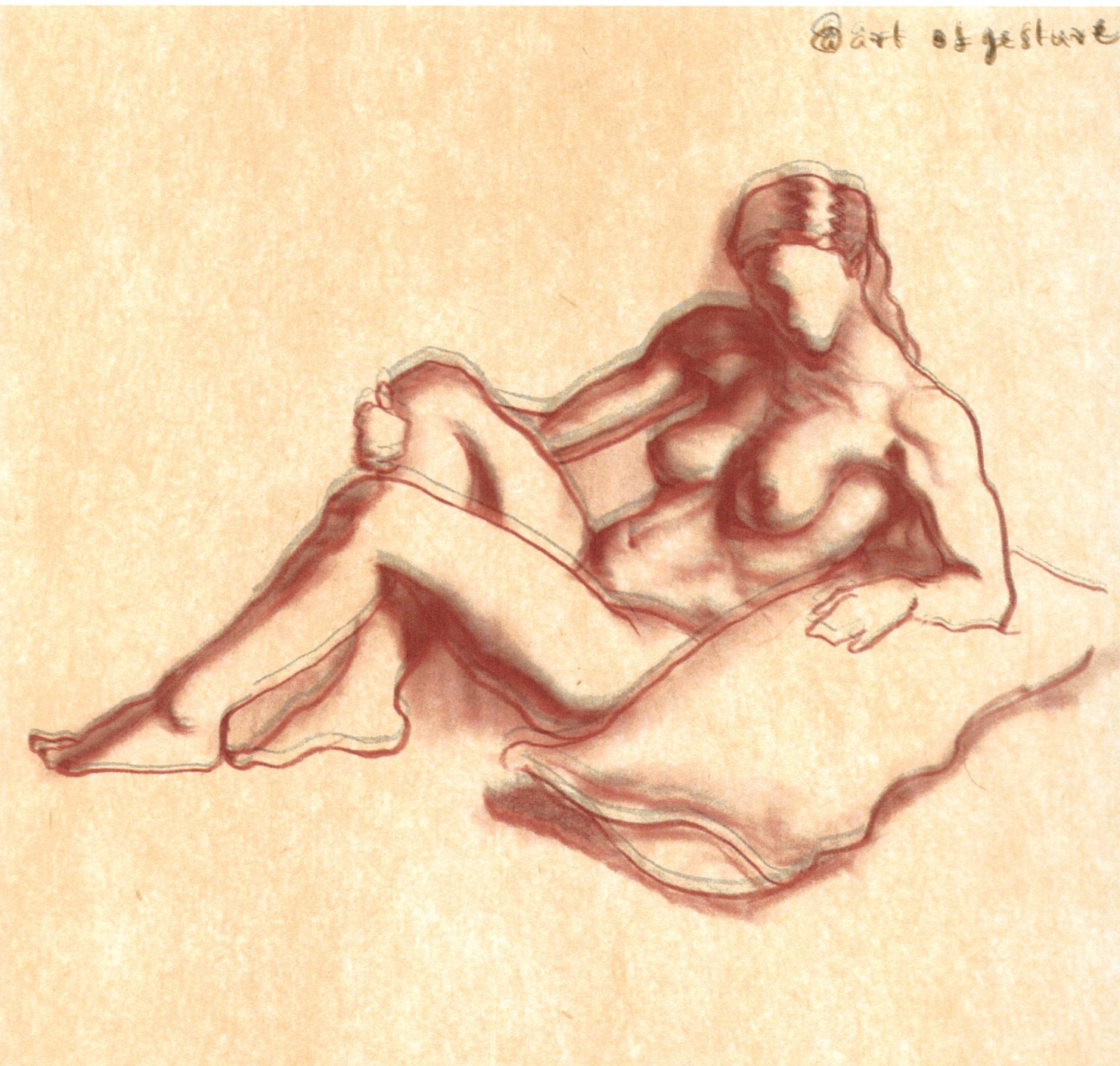

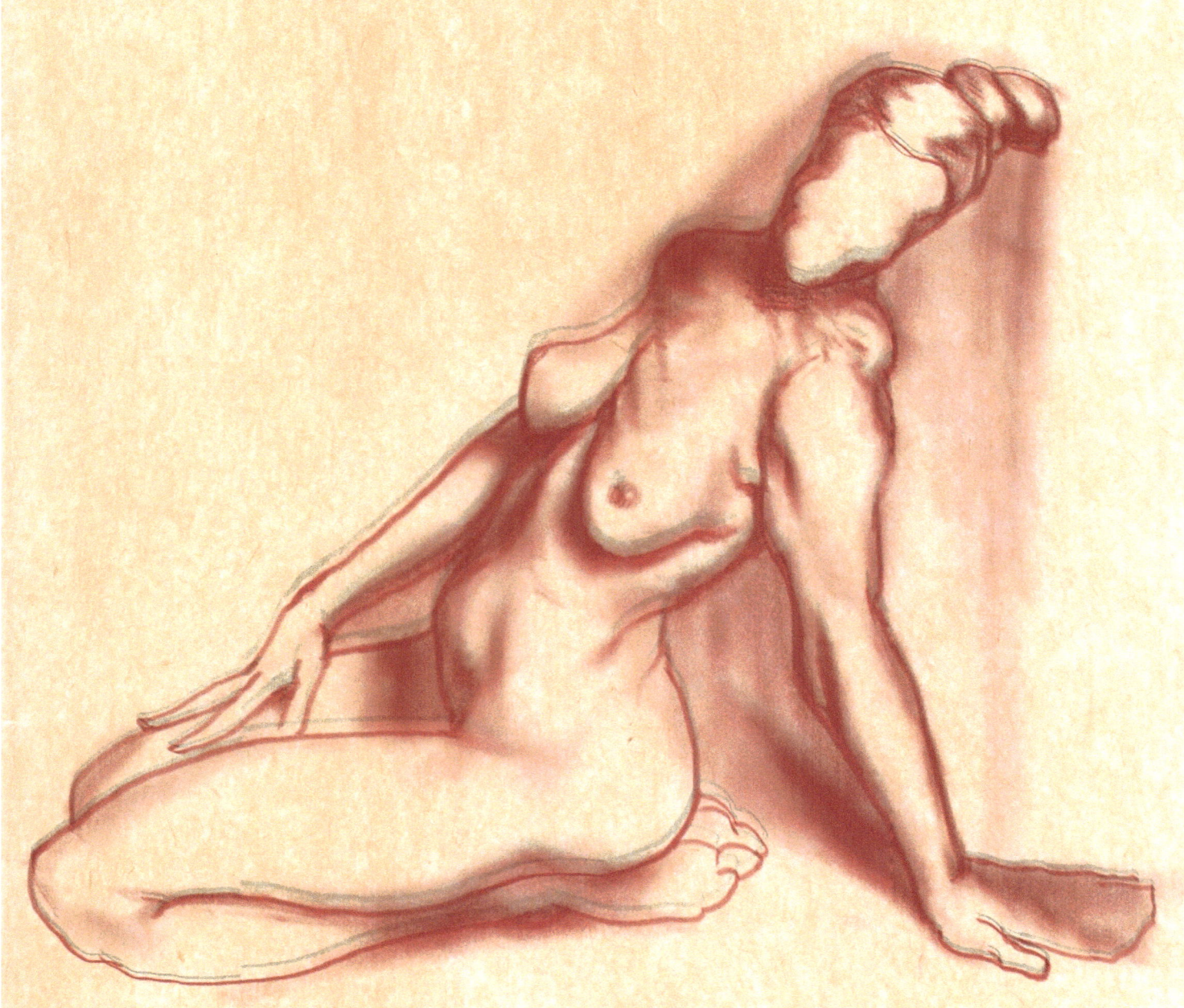

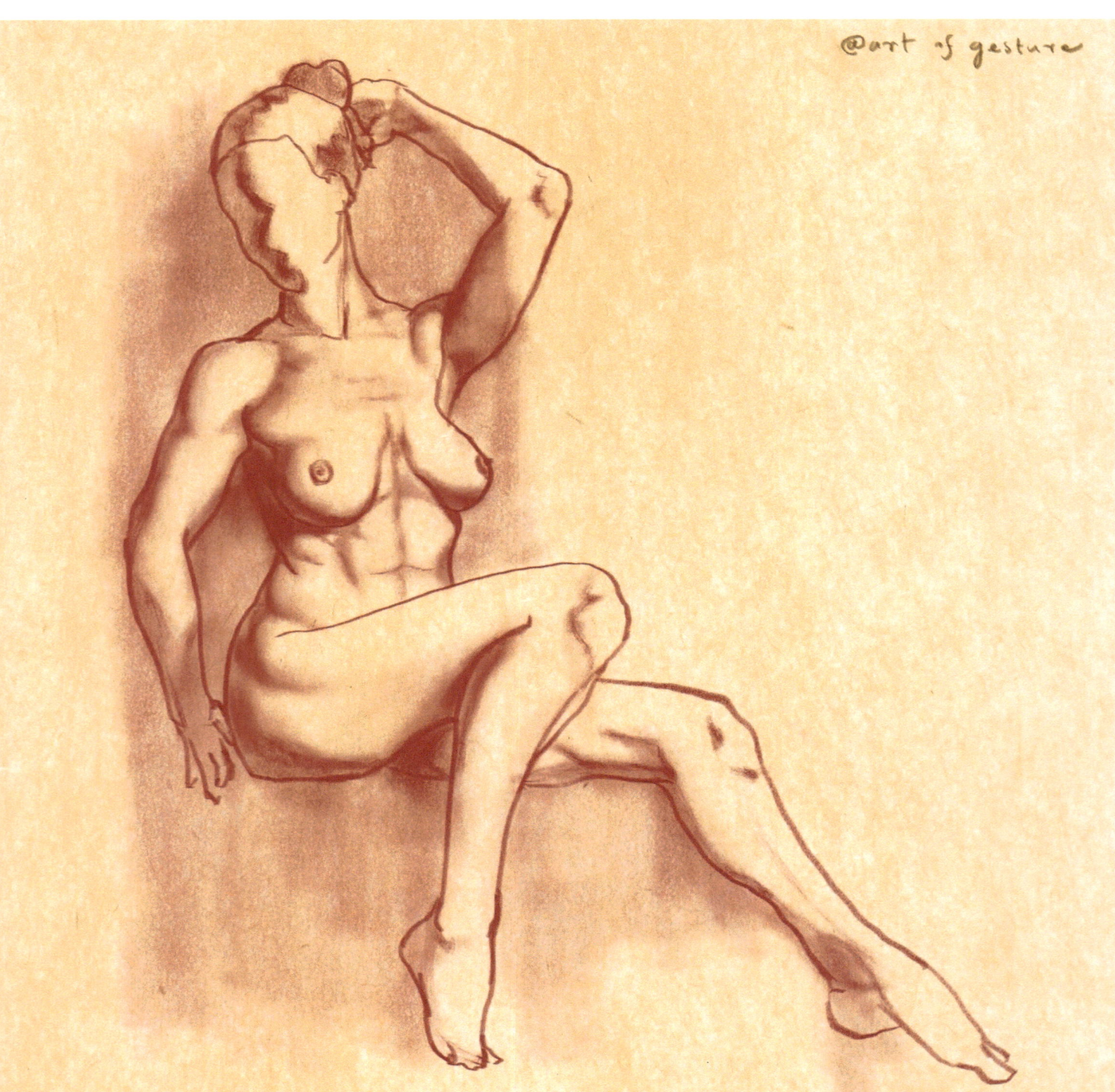

©art as gesture

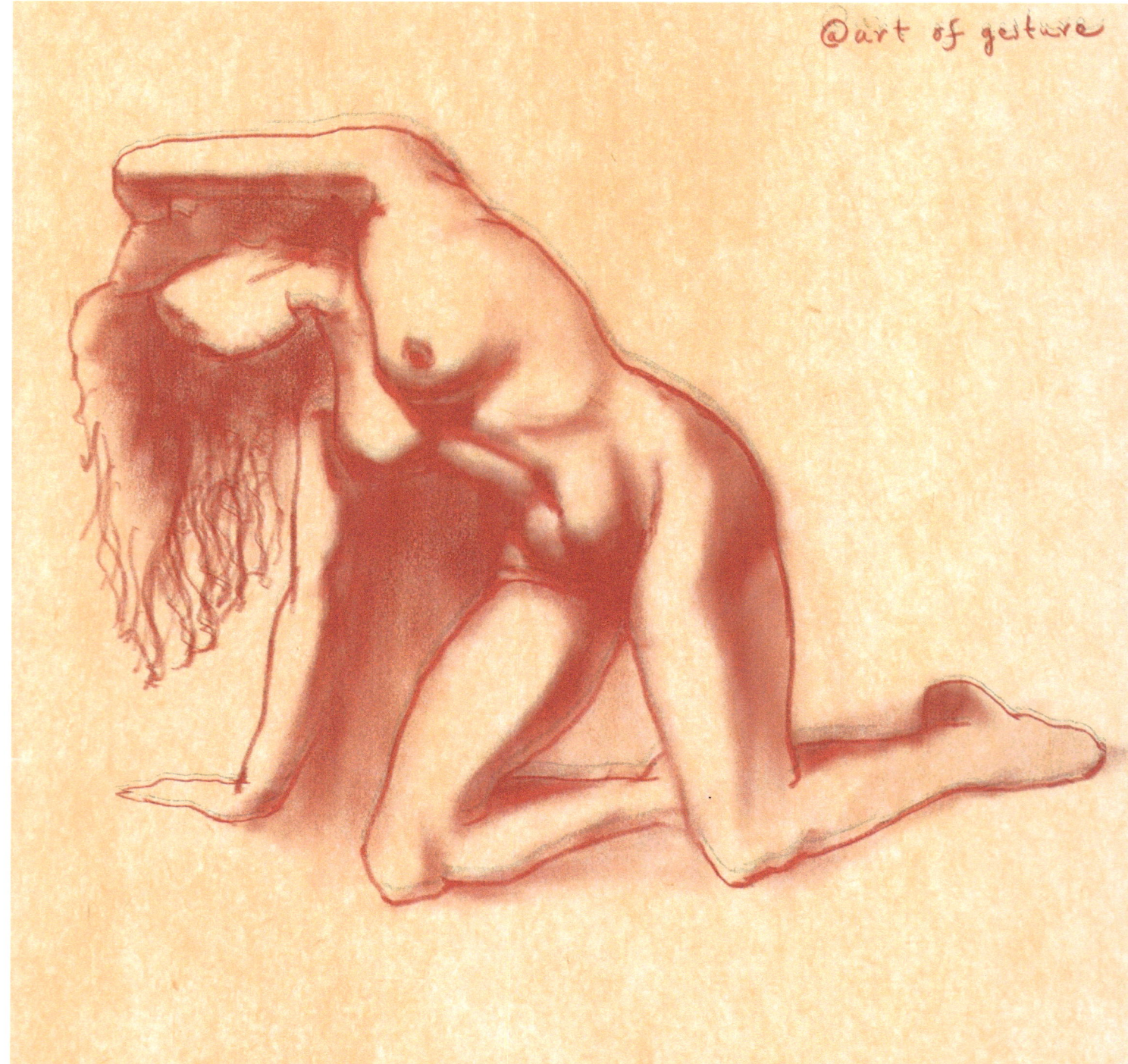

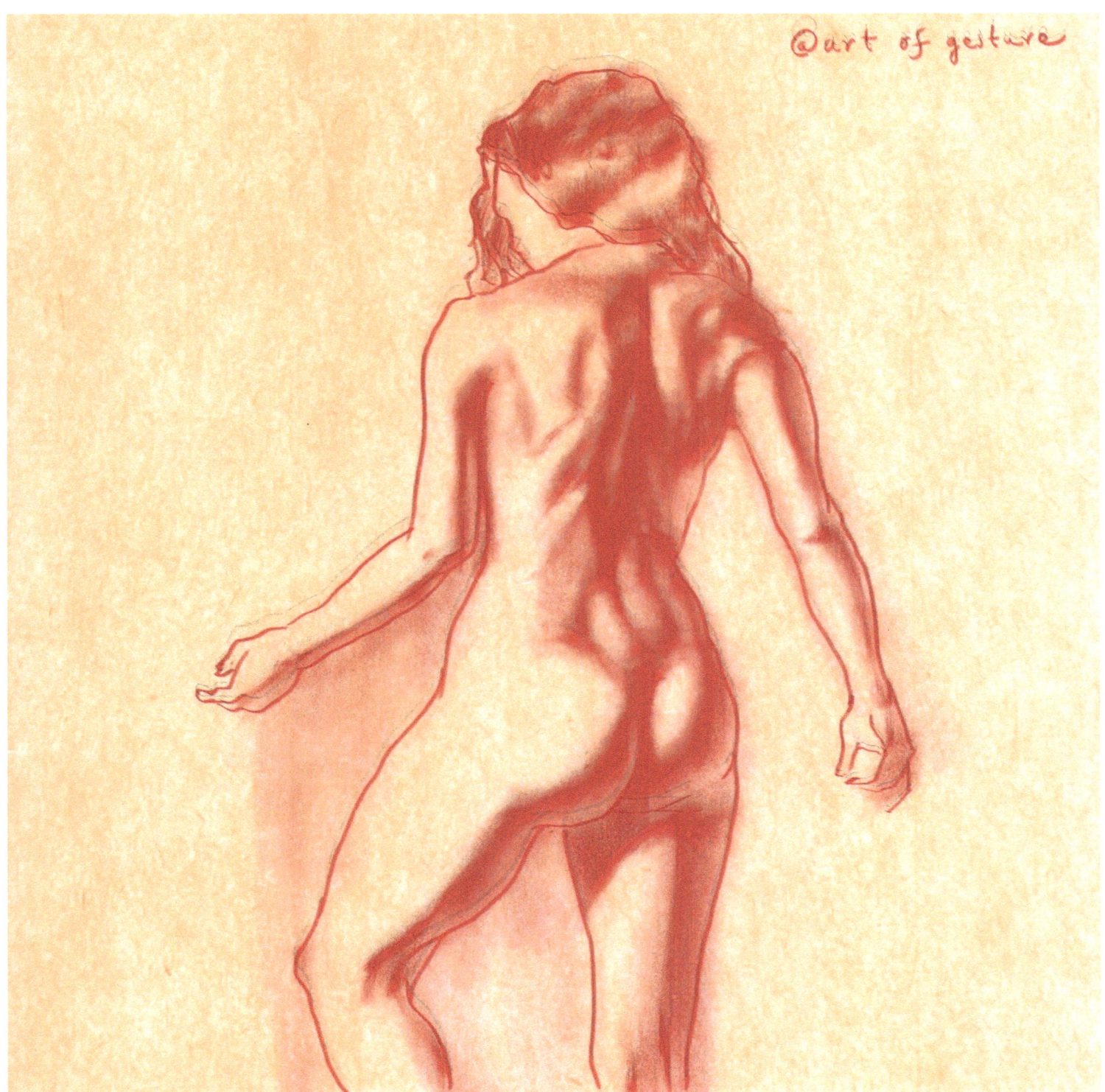

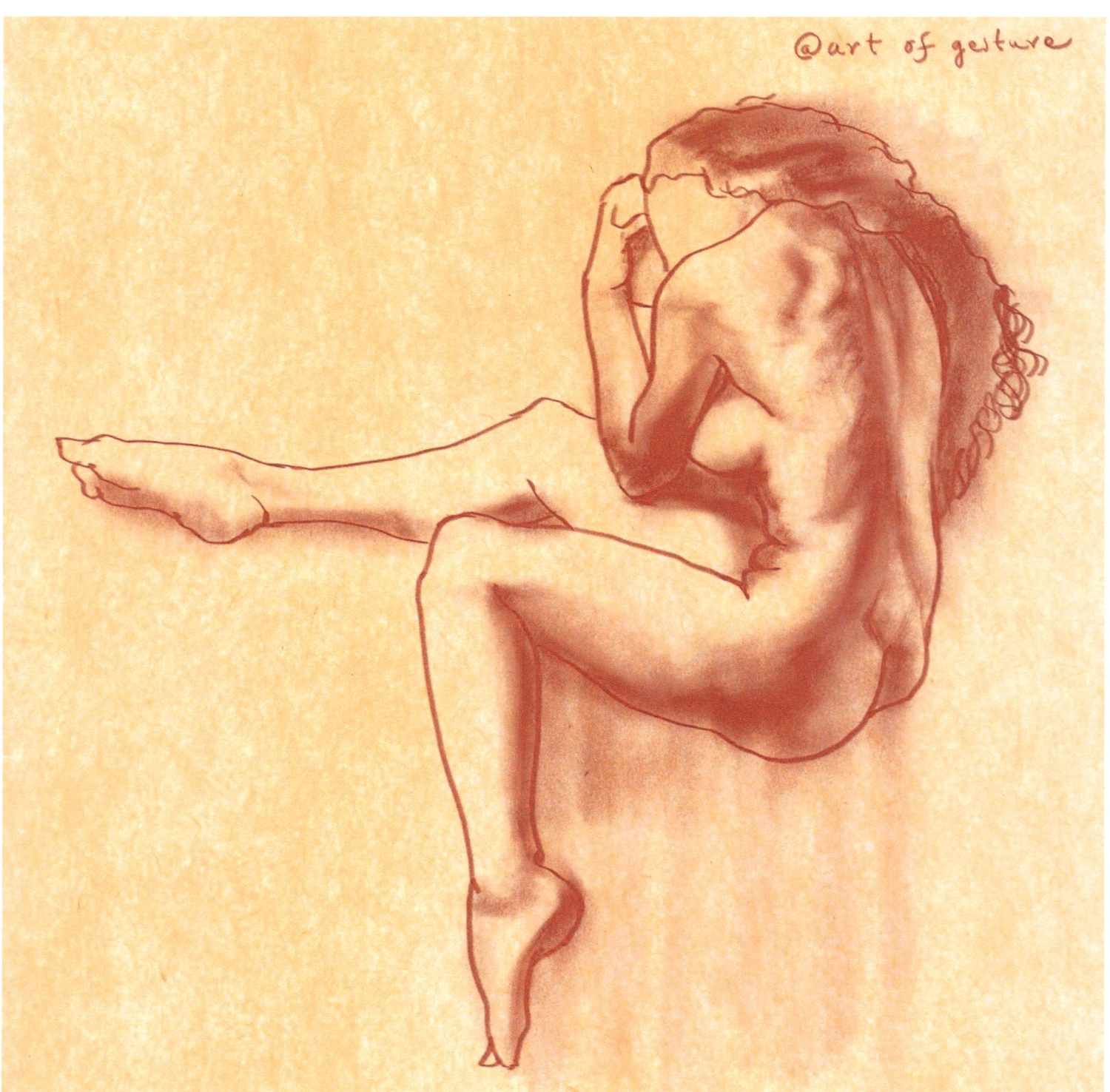

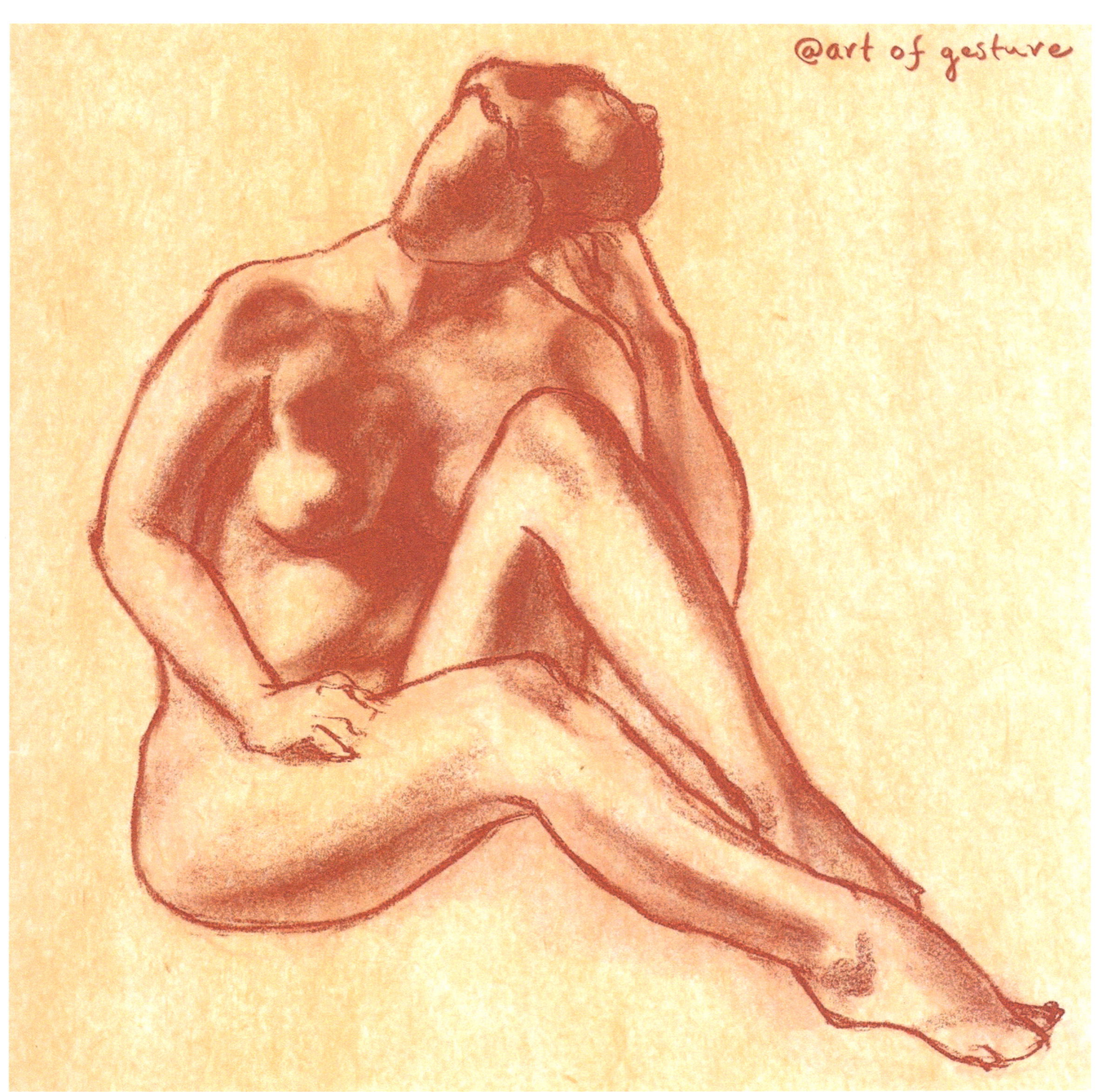

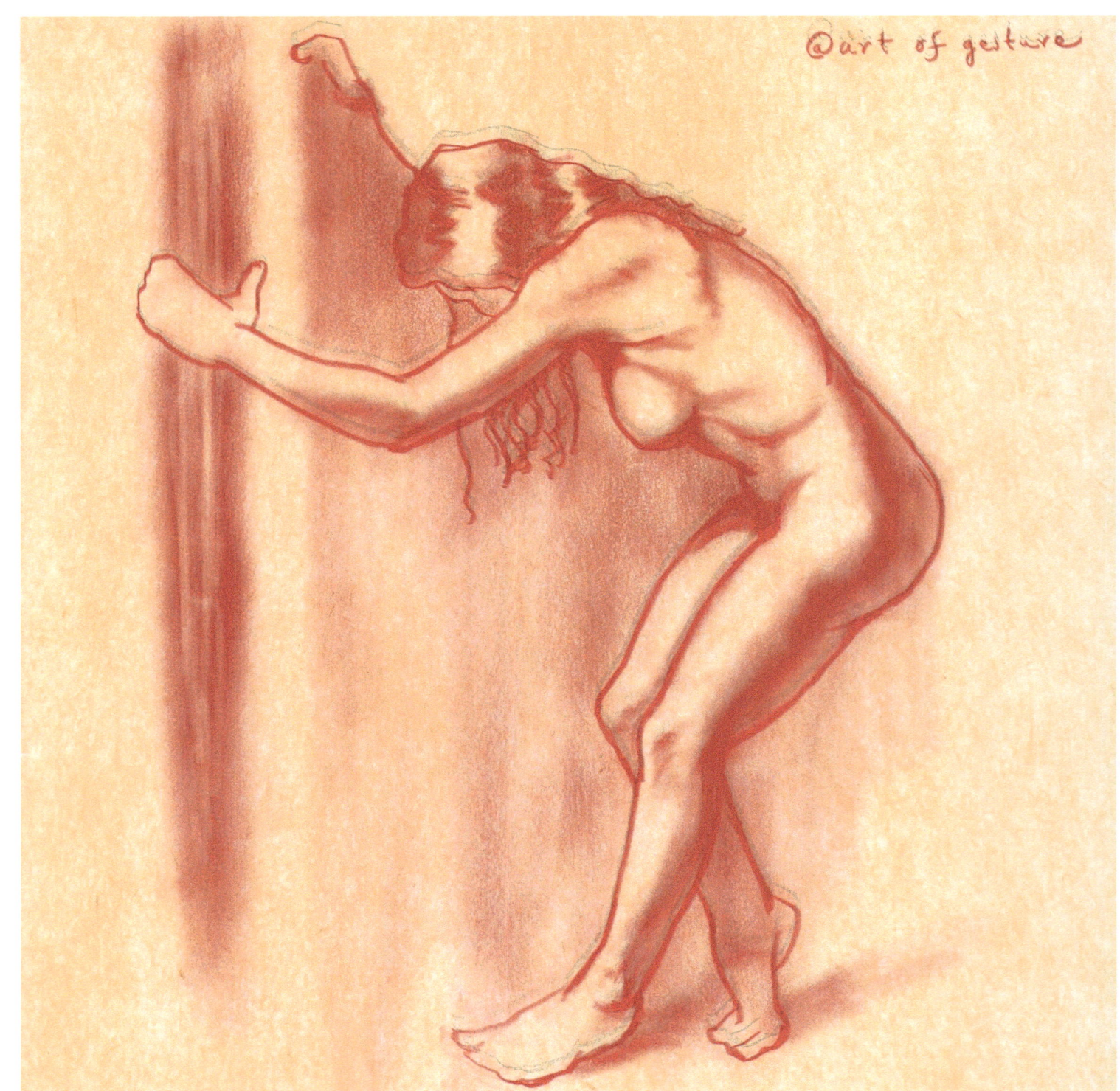

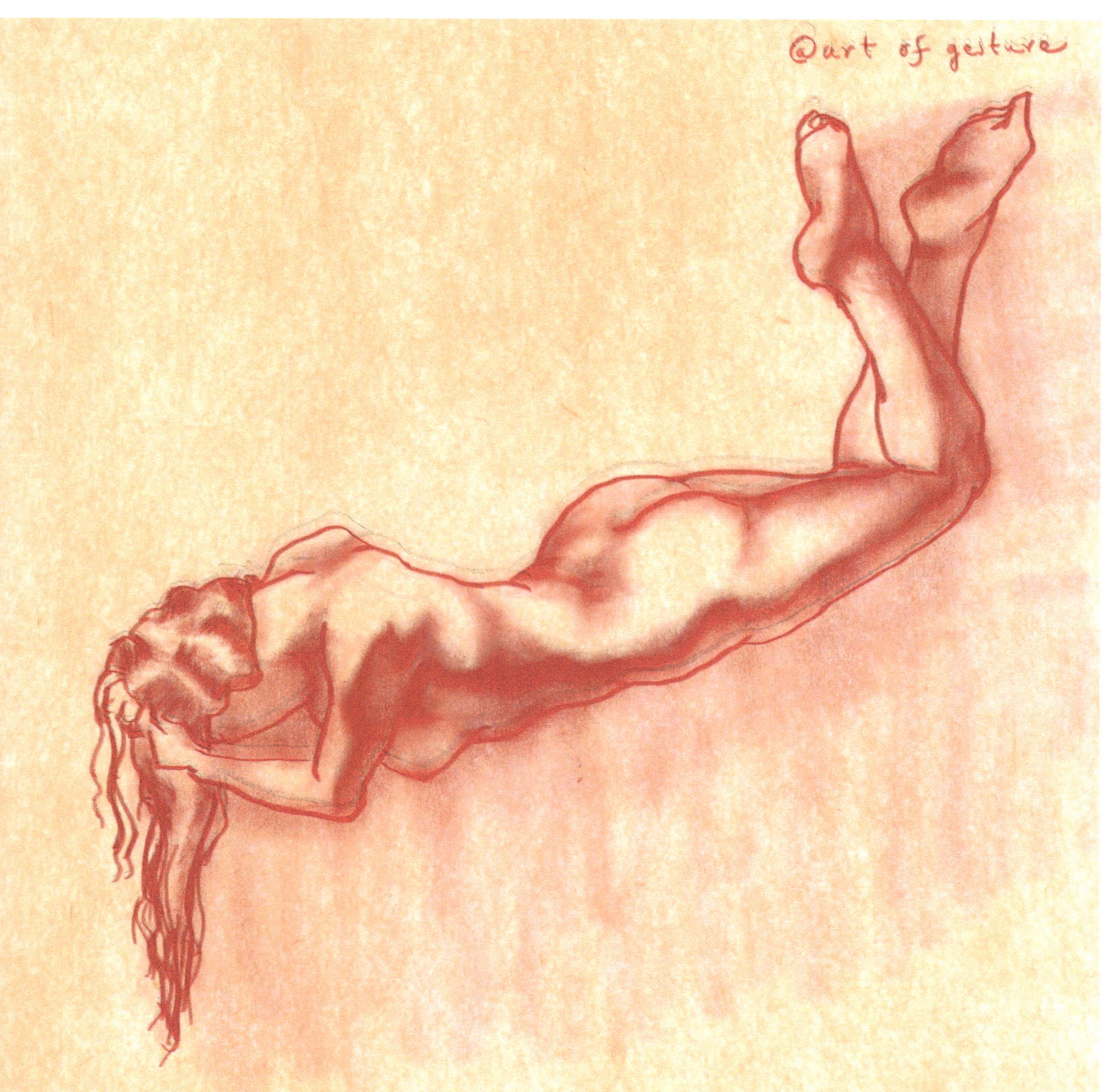

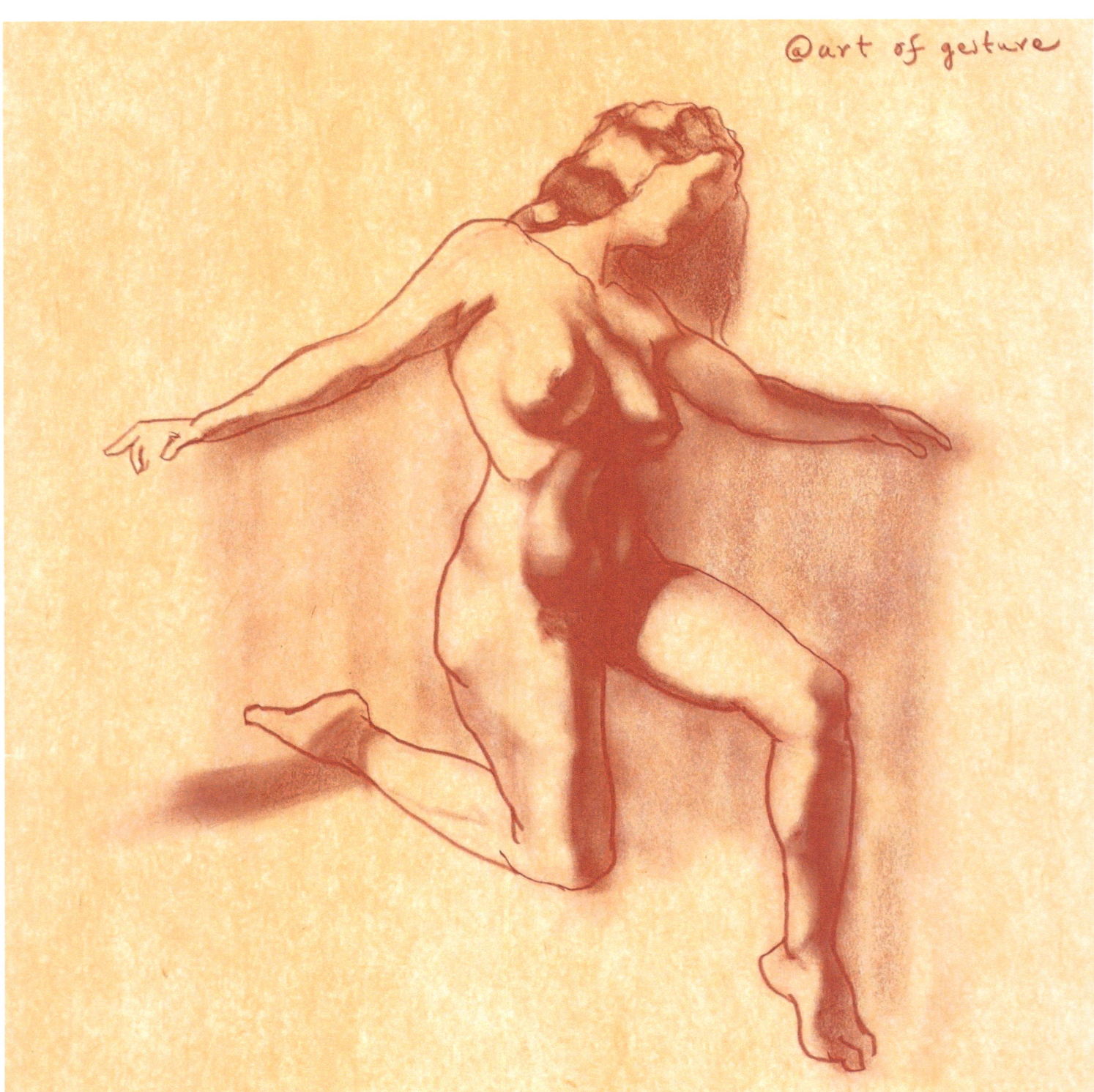

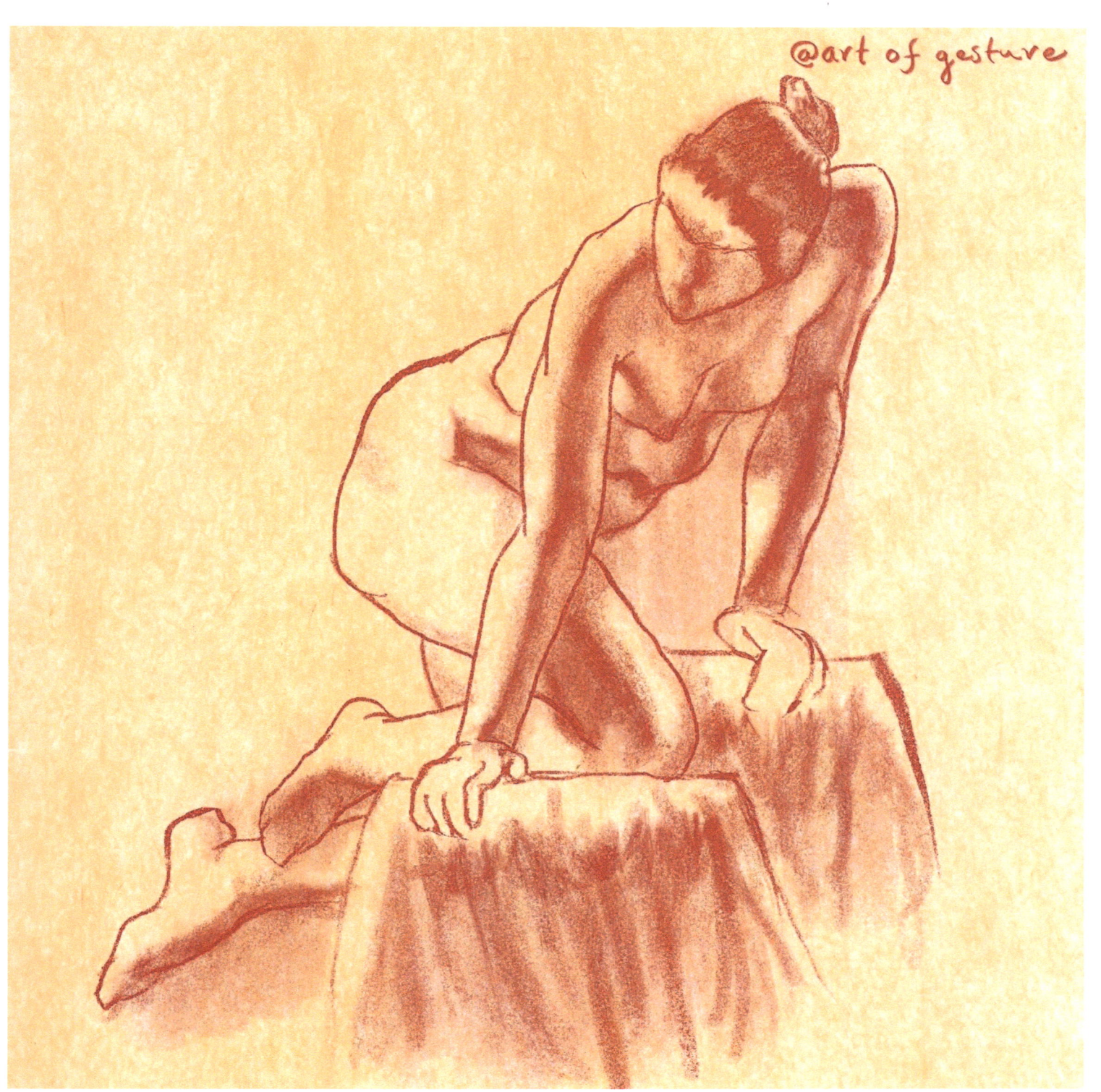

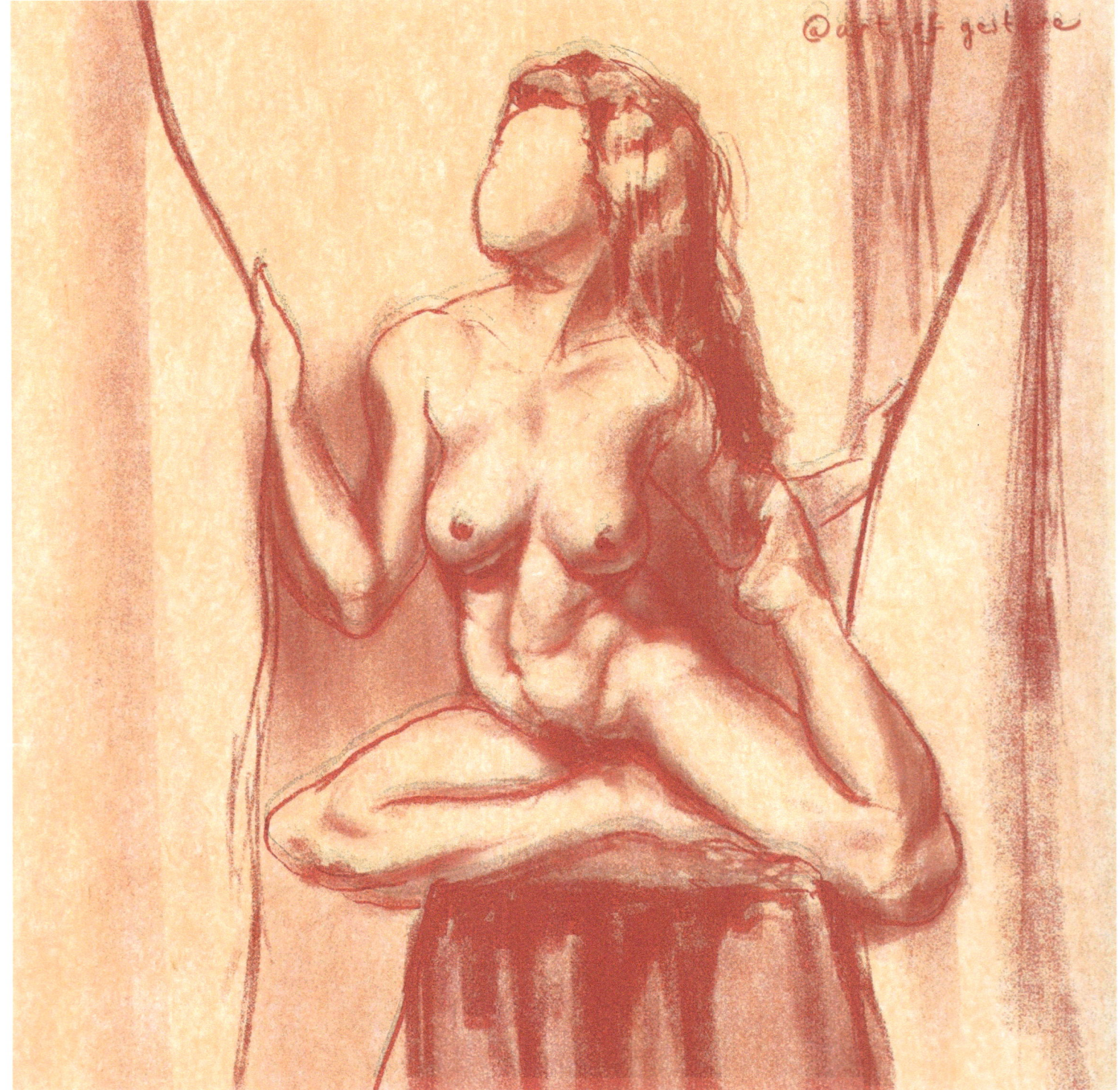

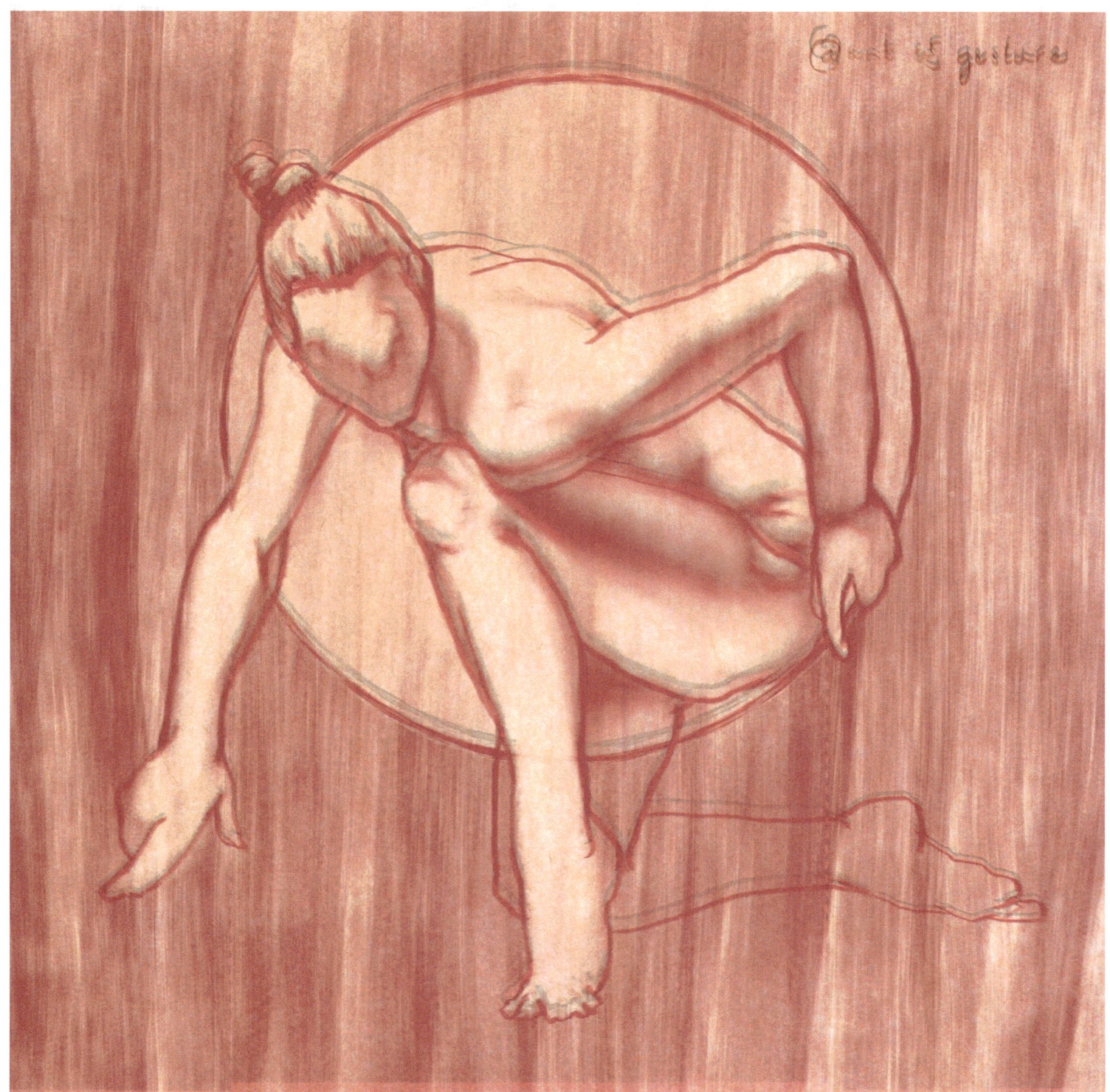

Process

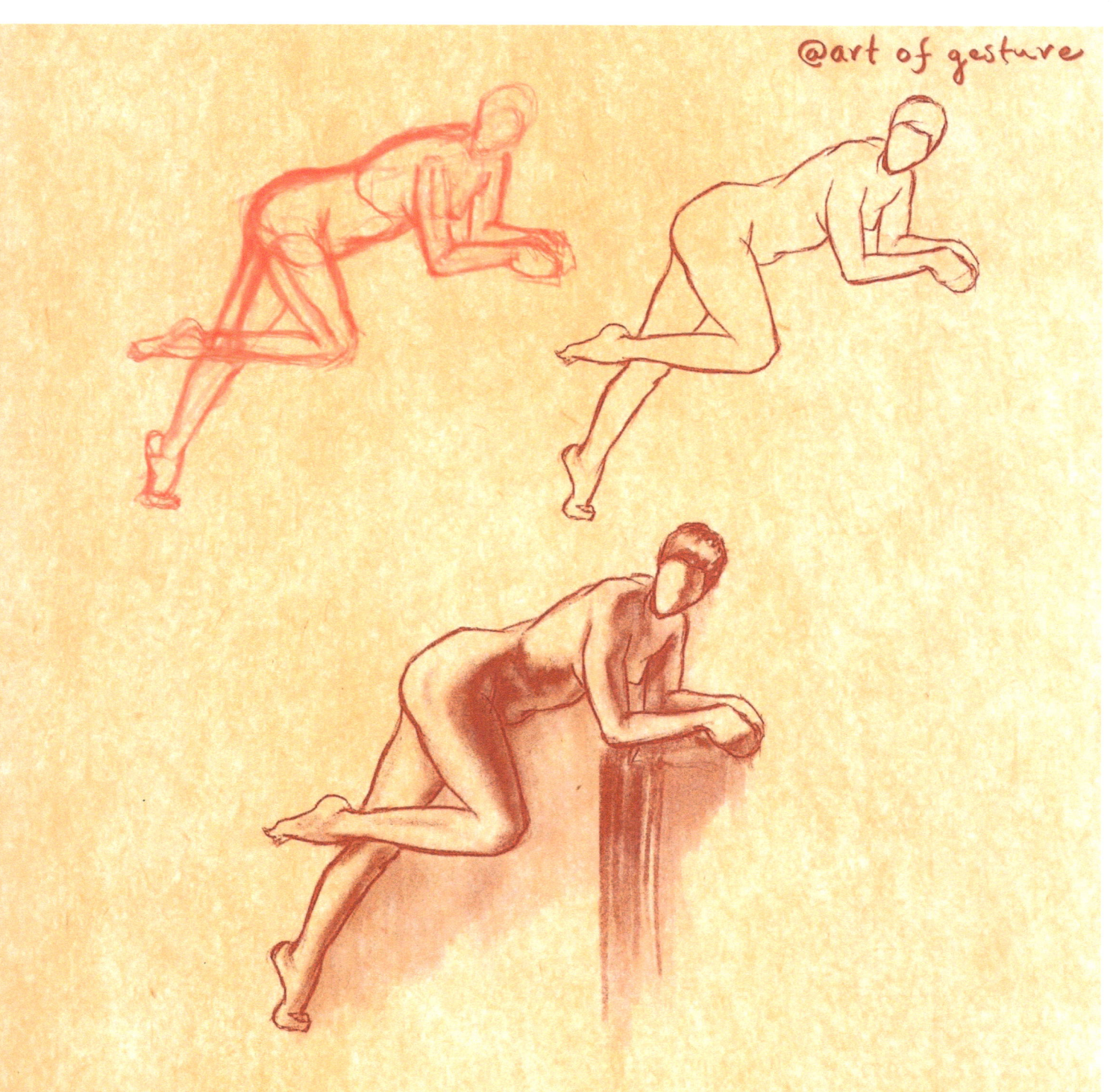

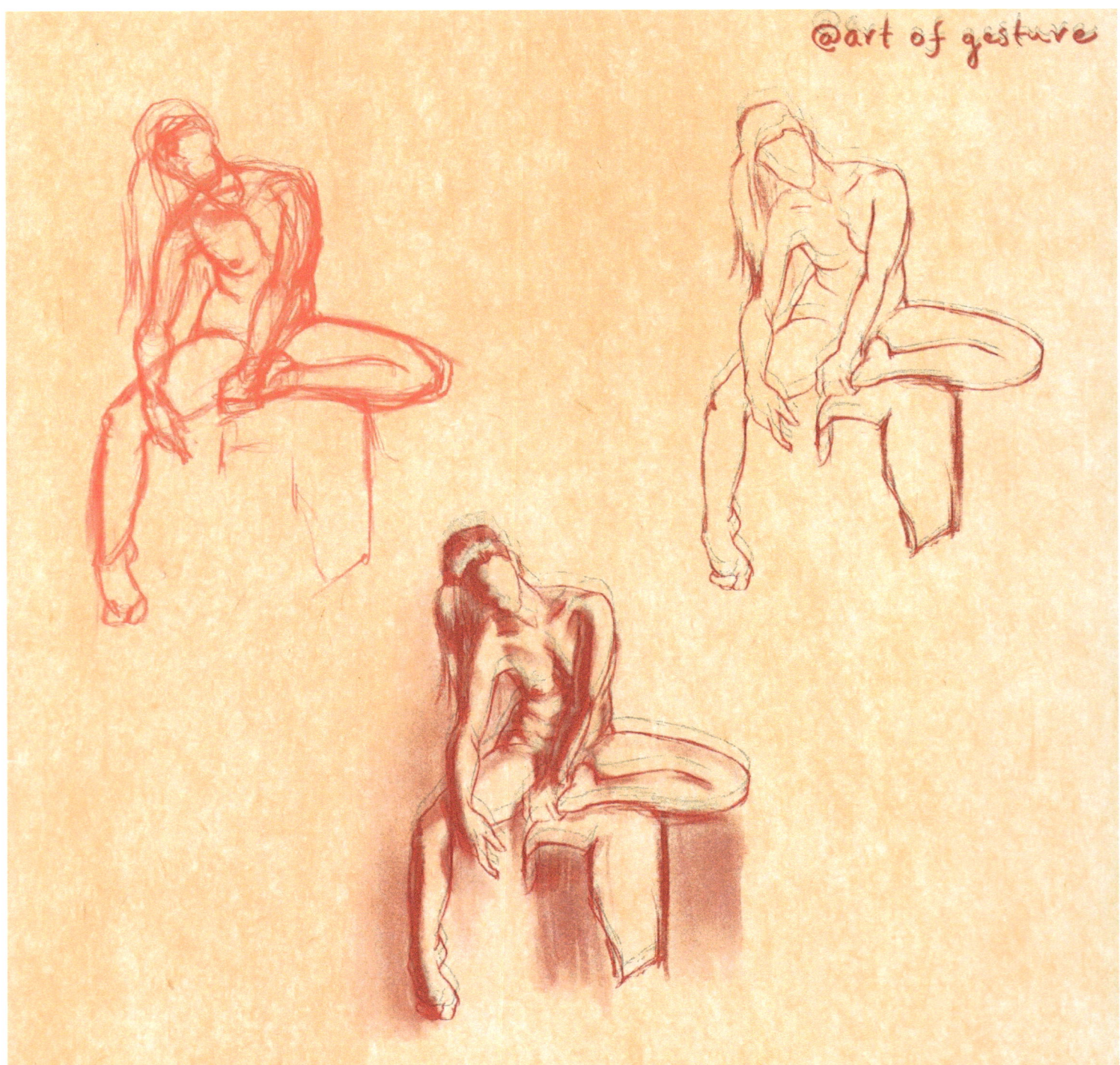

Afterword

Hello everyone,

I am a self-taught artist. I am software engineer by profession and I draw during spare time in my 12 hour work schedule. I had to discontinue my passion due to long travel to work place.

COVID-19 came as blessing in disguise which allowed me to cut down travel time and get back to my passion. I restarted my passion and opened Instagram account @artofgesture. The main objective was to push myself to draw daily for a minimum of 40 minutes.

I recently completed 100 days non-stop streak with minimum 2 posts per day. I hit 1000 followers in just over 100 days. The journey was not easy, there was big learning curve involved with a lot of hurdles.

Coming from a conservative society where there are no life drawing sessions, I attended my first life drawing session virtually. My mom contracted corona, there were many sleepless nights. And cherry on the top, I have a baby coming next year.

Despite these difficulties I kept going. Here I am, a testimonial that we can capitalize on any difficult situation if there is passion. I owe my sincere thanks to many online sessions where I met many amazing artists and models who kept me going despite in this difficult time. My thanks to my family, friends and to you who has made my journey sweeter.

Love,
Bharad

@artofgesture

artofgesturedrawing@gmail.com